Accountants and Other Daredevils

Also by Carol Patterson

The Business of Ecotourism
Saving Paradise: The Story of Sukau Rainforest Lodge
Reinventure: How Travel Adventure Can Change Your Life

Accountants and Other Daredevils

Unlocking Your Inner Superhero

By Carol Patterson

Order this book online at www.trafford.com
or email orders@trafford.com

Most Trafford titles are also available at major online book retailers.

© Copyright 2011 Carol Patterson.
All rights reserved. No part of this publication may be reproduced, stored in a retrieval
system, or transmitted, in any form or by any means, electronic, mechanical, photocopying,
recording, or otherwise, without the written prior permission of the author.

Printed in the United States of America.

ISBN: 978-1-4269-0803-3 (sc)
ISBN: 978-1-4269-0804-0 (e)

Trafford rev. 12/08/2010

 www.trafford.com

North America & international
toll-free: 1 888 232 4444 (USA & Canada)
phone: 250 383 6864 ◆ fax: 812 355 4082

To my mother, a daredevil for eight decades

Table of Contents

Acknowledgements

An Attitude of Gratitude is something I live by (or try to) and I felt extremely grateful as this book took shape. Thanks to Hope Bishop for shaping my wandering thoughts into concepts that put a spring in my step. My editor, Don Morberg, offers as much wisdom over pizza as an oracle on the mountain, and with much less climbing. He is the word superhero needed by every daredevil with a pen.

Thank you to Kayleen Newsom for launching me and my iMAC, and for stopping me from launching it out the window mid-book. Dave Maryka was another godsend, enhancing my digital capabilities and showing me how a book can come to life with video.

My greatest thanks go to my husband Colin for his unwavering support as I unlocked my closet superhero. His willingness to overlook a few false leaps and misplaced kryptonite gives me poise for new adventures.

Unlocking Your Inner Superhero?

What It Takes

Ever wondered what goes through a superhero's mind when she makes that first leap off a tall building?

"Whoa! That's a long way down!"
"Hope those flying lessons pay off!"
"Why did I ever start this?
"No going back now!"
"Do these tights make my butt look big?"

I know because I took that leap. I walked away from a successful career as an accounting executive in the oil and gas industry to follow my dreams. I wanted a way to combine my love of animals and adventure travel with a lifestyle that didn't include recycling bottles to pay the rent. So I considered my options and my dreams, ignored the doubts of others and

I leaped off the building. And survived. Survived? No, I thrived. Plus I've seen others do it. Some on their own and some because their friends and family encouraged them.

Because I made that leap and I've seen and helped others do it, I know you can as well. I want to tell you how I did it and how others have successfully planned and executed their leaps. Perhaps you can find some inspiration in the stories to help you start preparing for your own leap.

Luckily for me, when I made my leap I landed on a plane. I had been volunteering at the Calgary Zoo as a docent, so I leveraged that into what I called the Flying Zoo program. I took whatever animals would fit into a Cessna 172 to visit children in rural communities. Sort of an exotic petting zoo that comes to your town. The lessons I learned as the Zoo's first pilot eventually led to my role as Chairman of the Zoo's Board of Directors and, from there, a new career as an ecotourism consultant, author, teacher and public speaker.

Today, I am still flying. Now you'll find me flying economy class to emerging tourism destinations. As president of Kalahari Management Inc., a strategic planning firm, I help people identify what they can offer tourists and the steps needed before welcoming the world. I have been chased by elephants, waded ankle deep in cockroaches in Borneo, hobbled across Bhutan on a broken ankle, and nearly froze to death on a llama safari; but I have found a way to do what I really want to do in life.

The lessons didn't stop with the Flying Zoo program. In my adventures, I have met many other people, daredevils if you will, who have overcome tremendous obstacles to live the kind of lives that have people saying, "I wish I could do that!"

I have noticed some things that these emerging superheroes have in common. In general, these daredevils are connected to their community, embracing change in their businesses, and inspiring their children. If they are business people, they are not just balancing debits and credits; they are enhancing the social fabric where they live. They are treading lightly on the planet. They are the superheroes balancing a triple bottom line, even with a run in their tights or a cape that doesn't quite fit.

And the best news? You can be a daredevil too! Learn how to combine your professional training or experience with your special interests to live your best life. You don't need to quit your job or move to Mongolia. You can break from the crowd and create unique opportunities for yourself and others while living your everyday life. Things may look the same on the outside but you will feel different inside.

In this book I want to share the humorous and inspiring stories of people who are making tracks and making a difference. The lessons they share will awaken the daredevil in each of us.

How I Got My Cape

A funny thing happened to me on the way to becoming a Park Ranger. I ended up as a professional accountant! How did I manage to end up counting beans when I wanted to be counting bears? You see, I've always been a huge animal lover and my earliest memories are of me playing animal trainer with my friends and siblings.

I would convince my younger playmates that they should pretend to be horses or dogs or elephants while I would be the animal trainer. "We never had a lawn chair to sit on for several years," my mom recalls, "They were covered in blankets and turned up-side down to become barns or whatever imaginary setting the kids were creating that day."

My love of animals extended to wild animals and traveling to see them. Every summer vacation we packed the car and headed to the Rocky Mountains. We camped because it was an affordable way to travel, not for any great love of canvas tents or wet sleeping bags, although we experienced both.

The best part of visiting Canada's national parks was the interpretative programs. Every campground had campfire talks; and I remember sitting, transfixed, as some keen Park Ranger swatted mosquitoes and told stories. I hoped one day I would wear a Parks Canada uniform.

In Grade 12, I was delighted to discover a forest ranger program at Saskatoon's Kelsey College. I practically skipped home clutching the brochure describing classes on wildlife management, forestry and aquatic biology. Dreams met reality at the kitchen table.

"You don't like bugs, you get cold really easily, and living in remote areas like this wouldn't be a good career for a woman," said mom, dousing cold water on my dreams. With the benefit of thirty years hindsight, I can see she was right and probably saved me a lot of heartache; but at the time it was an abrupt return to earth. Kind of like finding out that Santa Claus wasn't real. But my parents were right about that too, so I figured I should take their advice.

A Misguided Guidance Counselor

Determined to research my other career options, I went to see the school's guidance counselor. "What subjects are you good in?" she asked. "Well, I've good math scores," I replied. With minimal effort, I had earned a 98% average in algebra and trigonometry; one teacher claimed he could use my exams as answer keys.

"You should be an accountant!" the guidance counselor declared. "What's that?" I asked. By the time I knew the answer to that question, I had a degree in Business Administration and another in Economics; it was too late to back out.

I started as an articling student for one of the "Big Five" Chartered Accounting firms, auditing financial records. I tackled challenging tasks like ticking and bopping. It sounds more fun than it is. Basically, you find invoices to support financial transactions and confirm the company, date and amount. The first time you do it, it's mildly interesting. By the end of your first month, you are reading recruiting brochures for the French Foreign Legion.

By year end I decided this was not the life for me. I felt at a primal level that I needed to make a difference to someone, somewhere. Every day I felt like the accounting cop, looking for problems and handing out citations. "Oh, oh, you've got the prepaid expenses over recorded!" This didn't seem like work that was going to change the world or at least mine.

After auditing, I tried an accounting job at a car dealership. It was more interesting than ticking and bopping, but again not very challenging. Because my husband at the time was in the Armed Forces, people were reluctant to hire me since they thought we'd be moving soon.

That problem resolved itself a few months later when my marriage crumbled, and I found myself driving a 1978 canary-yellow Pontiac Acadian to the land of milk and honey – Calgary. A former co-worker had offered me couch space while I looked for work; it seemed too good an offer to pass up. I packed two lawn chairs, a cot, sleeping bag, and ironing board for the big adventure.

Calgary was in the middle of an oil boom when I arrived. After the government-town culture of Regina, Calgary was a shock. Oil money flowed freely with lots of employee perks. Each evening, after handing out resumes, I'd hear yet another story of oil company largesse from friends, "They have free cookies and crackers in their lunch rooms," "They give bus passes to their employees," or "They get free gym memberships and every Friday afternoon off."

My current benefits included TV as I drifted off to sleep, so scoring an oil and gas job would mean a big step up. Unfortunately, my search wasn't going well. After three weeks I'd papered the town with resumes, but no one had asked for an interview. "I will have to come home this weekend," I told my mom. "Unless I can find something tomorrow, I will come back to Regina and wait for a call."

Feeling discouraged, I called an employment agency advertising for an accountant. That position was filled, but they asked if I'd applied at Dome Petroleum. "No," I said, "For some reason, I could never find their office in the middle of the chaos of Calgary's commuter train construction."

By the end of that day I had a job at Dome and a deposit on an apartment. "I'm flying home this weekend," I told my mom and dad, "I need to get some furniture!" This was the beginning of an exciting new chapter in my life.

Spreading My Wings

Working for Dome was like landing in the California gold rush, minus the gold and the dust. The company was growing rapidly and processes were created on the fly. If you volunteered to try something, you'd be given responsibility far beyond a 'normal' job.

I started in the Beaufort Sea division as a junior accountant, but I wasn't there long. I worked long hours and moved into budgeting, then systems design, and eventually leading others. Before I was thirty, I was supervising seventy employees and responsible for distributing hundreds of millions of dollars in revenue each year.

As fun as the perks and end-of-season parties were, I still wasn't satisfied. I met some fabulous people, many of whom are still close friends; but I didn't feel like I was making a difference. Also, I wasn't working with animals, unless you counted the drunken antics at the Christmas party.

Fortunately, I'd been building a parallel life. With few friends when I first moved to Calgary, I spent my Sundays lurking where I did find animals – at the Zoo. I watched the animals, attended special programs, talked to the staff and read the membership newsletters. The Zoo was starting a docent program to train volunteer interpreters. I figured the uniform looked almost as good as a forest ranger's and sent in my application.

I was nervous as I waited for my interview. "Will they will think an accountant has the social skills necessary to lead animal tours? We accountants don't exactly have a charismatic image," I muttered to myself. But they must have liked my style as my acceptance letter arrived in the mail soon after.

I danced around the mailbox as if studying evening and weekends for a non-paying job, on top of a demanding paying one, was the best thing that could happen to a gal. Because for this gal, it was! My involvement with the Zoo was the start of a much bigger life change.

Zoo School

Docent school was everything I hoped it would be and more. I learned taxonomy and zoo history. I discovered how to run AV equipment and how to handle snakes, one of the ambassador animals. Being a snake handler wasn't on my bucket list, and I tried to make myself invisible the afternoon we learned those skills.

Brian Keating, then Education Manager, must have liked shrinking blondes, because he pointed to me and said," Here why don't you take Rosie?" as if I was the most eager-looking student he had. Either he needed glasses or I'm a bad actor, because I wanted to take that two-metre boa constrictor as much as I wanted the measles.

People say that fear of public speaking is second only to fear of snakes. I was lucky in that I used my fear of snakes to overcome my fear of public speaking. While holding Rosie I was too worried about whether she would bite a zoo guest or stick her tail up my shirt to fret about my speech.

Being extremely busy at work and tied up with zoo work on evenings and weekends, I signed up for flying lessons. You can always make time for the things you really want or really want to do. Part of my work involved travelling to the Arctic, so I set aside that extra pay for the lessons. I had always been fascinated with airplanes. "I'd rather sit further up in the plane," I explained when a friend asked why I added flight school to my already-busy life.

With my new pilot's license, I soon got tired of doing touch-and-go landings at Springbank airport near Calgary. The Zoo had a Zoo To You program where docents took small animals to nursing homes and schools for education programs. Looking at that program, I came up with my own variation. Why not a Flying Zoo to You?

I pitched my idea to Brian Keating, inviting him out for a pitcher of Margaritas while I outlined by unorthodox idea. Before the first drink was finished, Brian, who was always looking for new and innovative ways to spread the zoo's messages, was onboard and the Flying Zoo program was born.

For three summers, I flew a rented Cessna 172 to rural Alberta communities with whatever animals would fit inside. I wanted to take the zoo to kids that didn't get to Calgary often. Lizards, owls, porcupines and snakes were packed up and loaded onto the plane.

The Manager of the flying club would joke, "Make sure you take all the snakes out or I won't be able to rent that plane again!" So I had 'snakes on a plane' long before the movie came out. The largest animal I took was Sarah, a Binturong, or Malaysian bearcat. She was almost six feet from the tip of her nose to her tail. She had a musky odor made worse by her occasional airsickness. When we landed, I always had to hose her down on the tarmac, a service not offered by many airlines!

A Life-Changing Trip

I eventually tried another type of flying with the zoo, booking an African safari through their ecotourism program. "I've always dreamed of seeing Africa," I told my parents, "Once I've got this out of my system, I'll settle down and become a 'normal' accountant." It turns out I was lying like a sheet, because I've been to Africa seven times since, and also to many of the world's most out-of-the-way places.

What I discovered was a new form of tourism where people have fun on educational vacations in the wilderness. Ecotourism, as it was dubbed, could help local communities and provide impetuous for conservation of animals. This was a turning point in my life. I was fascinated by the concept of travel for a purpose; it was a way I could combine my love of animals, travel and conservation, without having to get too cold or buggy!

On that first safari, I had seen my future. I spent my time after I returned figuring out how to work in this field. I started out doing it wrongly, applying for jobs at safari camps in Africa; but never made a connection. Slowly I realized this work could be done in North America, but I wasn't sure exactly how. I did know that when I found out, a major change was coming to my life. I enjoyed my evening and weekend work more than my day job, so it was also becoming clear to me I needed a new job.

Taking a first, unsure step, I approached my employer about working in the company's international operations.

It wouldn't be ecotourism, but I thought the overseas experience and connections would be helpful. "You're a woman and you're too senior," my boss said, dismissing any chance of me making the move. I knew the door was closing on that stage of my career. I didn't want to do more of the same, so I knew it was only a matter of time before I left.

I started exploring university courses, looking at an MBA in tourism. I discarded that idea when I realized the first three-quarters of the program repeated my courses in business and economics. I was attracted to the geography program where I could explore tourism and resource management. These were day classes, so it looked like studying while I kept working was not an option.

I remember the moment when I realized I needed to quit my high-paying, high-opportunity job. I was feeling burnt-out after a the company went through a long merger with another company and I always felt on the verge of crying. I talked to a friend who had been through a similar process and I asked her how she had survived. "Things started getting better when I quit," was her reply. In that instant, I knew that was my solution. I had to put on the cape and jump off the building.

The logical part of my brain resisted, but my gut told me it was the right thing to do. Without a change, I was afraid I was headed to breakdown. I planned to work until September until school started. Instead I encountered yet one more of those corporate moments that frustrate, and instead of shrugging it off like people normally do, I did what people often wish they could do. I quit! My new husband left for work that morning married to an oil and gas executive, and came home to a soon to be unemployed future ecotourism expert.

With my days suddenly free, I enrolled in the University of Calgary's Geography program and took class after class tourism and world regions. I had taken a geography class during my first degree and loved it. I would have chosen geography then as a major if I had discovered it in my first year. So here I was, a decade later, gleefully immersing myself in social geography. I was the third oldest student in class, but I figured better late than never and got down to studying.

Serendipitous Moments

For one term paper I researched tourism impacts on employment in Drumheller, Alberta. During an interview with the town's economic development officer, he said, "If you want to do more research in this area, I could provide a small amount of funding." I didn't realize at the time how rare these opportunities are, but I wasted no time hightailing it back to my professor with the offer.

My prof, Dr. Dianne Draper, is one of those rare gems with the energy and desire to answer questions and 'work the system' to help her students. When I explained the offer I had received, she was immediately supportive. "We can set a self-directed course so you can do the project and get credit for your research," she said. I got down to work, interviewing hotel and restaurant owners and learning about the real world of tourism. I felt like a true social scientist when I discovered girlfriends and wives of inmates at the local penitentiary were an important part of the local labor pool.

"This is really good," Dianne said, when I handed in my paper, "You should enter a research competition." I didn't think I was ready, but I'd come a long way listening to wise advice, now was not the time to stop. I submitted my paper and was astounded when I received second place, euphemistically called the Merit Award. Even though I was the runner-up, I was thrilled to have my work recognized.

With my degree completed, I knew I wanted to work in tourism destination planning. Unfortunately, it looked like creating a career in this field was going to be tough going. There was one tourism development company in Calgary and it was in the process of shutting down. So, calling up those research skills I had honed at University, I started doing informational interviews with any tourism professional who would give me twenty minutes and their opinions on the current issues and trends.

Creating Kalahari Management

Over time, I concluded there were some parts of the tourism industry that I had no interest in, like hotels and golf courses. I was still determined to focus on ecotourism so it looked more and more like I would have to start my own company. One step closer to leaping off that building. I'd never seen myself as an entrepreneur, but I would have to quickly develop some Donald Trump-like characteristics if I was going to follow my dreams and make the mortgage.

I created Kalahari Management Inc., hung out my shingle as an ecotourism consultant, and started looking for my first client. I was a new company in a new field dealing with new clients who didn't know help was available or how it could help them.

It was tough. It took time to identify who was my market. I had met many ecotourism business owners who had a passion for the outdoors or paddling or bird watching, but detested the business side of things. I felt I could help them; I had a great business background and shared their love of wild places.

Unfortunately, many of them needed my help, but couldn't afford me. I learned there were government agencies helping these businesses and they became my clients. I was able to help the entrepreneurs, but found organizations with sufficient funding to make it happen.

Visionary or Crazy?

My parents weren't too sure about this leap into financial insecurity and wondered aloud when I might pick up a 'real' job. My husband, bless his heart, was always encouraging and took a 'que sera sera' view. Some of my former coworkers were shocked to hear of my plans. "Don't tell anyone you've left oil and gas to work in tourism, they'll think you are crazy," one fellow said. There were times when I thought I was too. I watched my friends buy bigger and fancier cars while I scraped together money to attend a tourism conference.

It was through tourism conferences that I built a network of people who would refer me to clients or hire me for projects. The work was, and continues to be, varied and challenging. People sometimes ask what exactly a tourism planner does, in the voice they might use to quiz the salesman at the front door. I explain, "I go to places before tourists discover them and help the people living there see what they have to offer, and get them ready to welcome the world." My focus has been on nature and ecotourism destinations, and it becomes very complex as you balance economic, social and environmental goals.

The travel I do is very rewarding, but it isn't as glamorous as some people think. Tourism businesses are busy during peak seasons, i.e. the good months, serving tourists. Tourism planning or market development work always occurs in the off-season, i.e. when the weather is bad!

I've become very good at imagining leaves are on the trees and birds are in the trees while wind and snow howl around my head. Since I work with emerging destinations, the accommodations aren't always what you see on the travel brochures. In the line of duty, I have stayed in a pig barn converted to a hotel, a retirement home, an old warden's cabin, a defunct school, a house in a fisherman's outpost home, and a ramshackle hunting cabin.

In a typical project I meet with community and government representatives, small business owners and guides to determine their tourism development goals. Most are looking for jobs and economic growth. Sadly, tourism is often seen as an economic engine of last resort once there are no more fish in the ocean, trees in the forest, ore in the mine or markets for grain. It is difficult convincing elected officials to commit five years to tourism investment when they face re-election in three; but I'm learning to look at change from a generational perspective, and not project to project.

Once goals are set, I will do a tourism inventory and assessment. I need to know how many hotel rooms exist and how many I'd put someone I like into. I've seen a few hotels that are euphemistically called 'not tourist ready'. For people outside the tourism industry, it means you wouldn't board a dead cat there.

Project Challenges

Sometimes I'm surprised at how people overlook the great things they have to offer while flogging something that has a limited market or no way to generate profit. One community thought they could build their future on cemetery tours. Although I realized people were dying to get into cemeteries (bad pun intended), I could not see how you could make money from them. Would there be enough revenue from selling maps or souvenirs? I was skeptical.

Nature often provides the gems that get people to travel. Sometimes it is simple, like stargazing in a dark sky near a metropolitan area. Or a swamp that holds the last of a disappearing species, like the Ivory Billed Woodpecker. These attractions are the focus of the strategic plan and we outline the steps needed to improve infrastructure, develop marketing plans and upgrade the labor pool.

One of my favorite projects was a plan to bring more bird watchers and nature lovers to Nevada. Most people associate that state with gambling and nightlife, but even successful destinations want to diversify. I worked on a team with Bob Garrison, Bob Barnes and Jeremy Garrett – each extremely talented in bird watching and market development – to identify where the opportunities might lie.

It was disconcerting to say the least, when we asked tourists if they had ever thought of visiting Nevada for its natural history, and hearing them say, "We drive through in the dark to avoid the heat." It is really hard to promote a tourism attraction if people go by when they can't see anything!

Fortunately, most bird watchers were willing to come when they heard more about Nevada. I was very proud when our study received an Excellence in Tourism Award from the Nevada Commission of Tourism. Nevada is one of the powerhouses in the tourism industry, outspending entire countries with their annual marketing budget, so being recognized by them felt very, very good.

I've also enjoyed my work in Northern Europe. I was introduced to the European countries ringing the North Atlantic by my associate, Dr. John

Hull. In one project, we helped Northeast Iceland increase its tourism visitation with a regional tourism strategy.

Iceland has done a wonderful job of establishing itself as one of the world's hottest cool destinations. My informal research shows that many people have Iceland on their bucket list and hope to visit once in their lifetime.

Iceland isn't easy to get to, but the government, in conjunction with Icelandic Air, has made it easier in recent years. You can break up your flight from North America to Europe on Icelandic Air with a stop in Iceland at no extra charge. Throngs of people have taken the chance to check out the geothermal activity by sightseeing, hiking or soaking at a spa.

Our job was to convince these people to venture further from Reykjavik and explore the mind-blowing beauty of the Northern coast. In conjunction with the Icelandic Research Center, we prepared detailed maps of tourism features and then grouped them into clusters. From there we created themes for product development and marketing. It was wonderful to see the small communities become stronger by embracing bird watching, spa experiences and farm tours.

Going to an emerging destination and discovering what is truly unique has unlocked my inner Sherlock Holmes. I find that being an outsider is invaluable, as sometimes people overlook the treasures while trying to copy tourism hot-spots. Open spaces, unique landscapes or rare combination of species attract nature lovers, and I am happy to show communities new to tourism how to unlock their potential with these markets.

Becoming an Author

Writing has become important for developing my business. I knew I would be writing business documents in my work, but early on I discovered that writing was a helpful way to establish credibility. I started a quarterly newsletter, *EcoTourism Management*. This was a great way to share the information I was discovering and to showcase the wonderful businesses I found.

Soon after I launched my company, I wrote my first book, ***The Business of Ecotourism.*** Although I didn't know any more when I finished the book than when I started, people thought I did! They bought the book to help their businesses or their communities as they built better nature or cultural-based products and it is still used around the world. The book also led to great speaking opportunities as people wanted to learn more.

At one of these presentations, I met someone who would have a lasting impact on my business. Albert Teo, founder of Borneo Eco Tours and Sukau Rainforest Lodge, invited me to speak at the Global Asia Pacific Ecotourism Conference in Borneo in 2002, the International Year of Ecotourism. In a gesture seldom seen, he invited me and the other speakers to Sukau Rainforest Lodge to recover from jet lag before the conference. If only all my speaking engagements were so interesting!

It was easy to spend two days in the Malaysian rainforest with Pygmy elephants munching at the river's edge for evening entertainment. I fell in love with this ecolodge and vowed to return with my husband. The next year I went back and Albert broached the idea of writing a book together. "I want to share my experience so that other people can learn from me and not repeat my mistakes," he said.

I agreed immediately and work started on ***Saving Paradise: The Story of Sukau Rainforest Lodge***. It was surprisingly easy to collaborate on a book across the world and the book was released to much fanfare in 2005. Borneo remains one of my favorite places and I've steered more than a few tourists to its ecotourism attractions.

Albert and his team gave me one of my most treasured accolades when they named me to the Kinabatangan Fellows of Conservation for recognition of my efforts to promote conservation in the Kinabatangan river basin. As one of this illustrious group, a room at Sukau Rainforest Lodge bears my name, although I have not been able to sleep in the Carol Patterson Room yet!

I've been fortunate to create a business that lets me work with communities and governments all over North America and beyond. I've traveled to places as varied as Borneo, Iceland, Scotland, Botswana and the Faroe Islands for work; and when I'm not traveling for business, I'm traveling for pleasure. With much of my time spent writing and speaking, my travel – whether it is for pleasure or work – blends together as I use the stories that

I find on the road to illustrate key concepts in my speaking and consulting projects.

Making It

Although I've got much to be proud of, I still work hard to get new contracts and there are always more ideas than hours to execute them all. It is the 'atta girl' moments that make it all worthwhile.

One of them came in 2007 when I received a Woman of Vision award by Global Calgary TV, The Calgary Herald and the YWCA. I thought I was a woman of insanity, but it turned out I was a woman of vision! In hindsight, insanity and vision are closely related. As you read this book, you'll see at the heart of any innovative organization lives at least one slightly crazed visionary, trying to do things that have never been done.

In 2011, I'll celebrate twenty years since I started Kalahari Management. It hasn't turned out exactly as expected, but in many ways it is better. I'm grateful now that I came to this work via accounting. When times are slow in tourism – think post 9-11 – I've been able to do project work that keeps me going until times pick up again. And I find it humorous that even though I do a lot of market research, I have more credibility because of my accounting background. Those people who warned me that I shouldn't tell anyone I was leaving oil and gas for tourism were wrong. In fact, the industry still claims me. The Society of Management Accountants profiled my career in their national magazine in December 2009. Adding cover girl to my list of accomplishments proved that following the road less traveled can lead to a person's greatest triumphs.

Can I Carry Your Luggage?

"Can I carry your luggage?" How I love to hear that question. My suitcase is usually heavy and full of books and cameras; it would be great to have my own Sherpa lugging my bags. My reality is that the budget barely covers the essentials like food and shelter; there is nothing in it for servants or travel companions.

But if I had a dime for every time someone has offered to come along on one of my trips or told me they want to do what I do, I could retire from consulting! "You have it made in the shade," one of my clients tells me. "Yes, I'm very fortunate," I agree, "but anyone can have a life like mine."

I wasn't born to great wealth and I didn't marry into money, so my unconventional life style was crafted by balancing my need to eat and my need to create and explore. If I can lead a fuller life, you can too!

I have learned much from leaping into the unknown and becoming a daredevil. Watching other trailblazers and the people setting the bar in complex organizations has taught me a lot about superheroes. They aren't just in comic books; they are as likely to be a mother of three as a young buff guy in spandex tights.

Times of crisis often bring out the unexpected heroes. Just read the newspaper after a natural disaster and you'll learn of ordinary people doing extraordinary things because they needed to be done. We don't have to wait for times of crisis to find superheroes and daredevils. Opportunities are all around us if you look. There is one inside of you. You just need some help in finding a phone booth (tough in this age of cell phones), sizing your costume, and discovering a reason to leap tall buildings.

I'm going to share the lessons I've learned from the daredevils I've met, and I bet you'll see yourself in one of them. You don't need to run away from home to be a superhero or keep a batmobile in the basement. You can start by looking up at what is possible, not down at the things holding you earthbound. You can move beyond feeling "is this all there is?" to "what a wonderful life!" You will know that your efforts matter, that your children admire you, and that you have made a difference.

Time for our first leap!

Lesson #1

Superheroes Are Attracted To Bright Lights

Superman lived in Metropolis, Batman in Gotham City, and Spiderman hailed from New York City. You'd be forgiven if you assumed all daredevils lived in big cities. While it is true that superheroes are more likely found in urban areas, just because of the population density, you'd be overlooking some amazing superheroes living, and fighting for, rural lifestyles.

As a tourism consultant, I'm asked to help rural areas develop as nature or cultural destinations. Many times this request comes out of desperation. The fish stocks have been depleted, the forests have been cut down, the mines have closed, or the main industries have moved offshore. In North America, the family farm is as endangered as Whooping Cranes.

Subsidies, low commodity prices and rising energy costs have pushed many people off the farm and out of their rural communities.

Migration patterns show an 'emptying out' of the middle of the U.S. as people follow jobs and warm weather to Nevada, Arizona and other southern states. As well, there are more people living in cities than in the country for the first time in history. This arrival of the Urban Millennium means daredevils residing in the countryside are getting scarcer.

Amongst the rural angst, there is reason to hope. Rural daredevils are working hard to revitalize their communities with economic initiatives based upon sustainability and partnerships. An example of one such effort can be found in southern Alberta.

After research showed European travelers were not likely to visit the Rocky Mountains twice, Alberta Tourism, Parks and Recreation asked if they would return to see the Canadian Badlands. The Badlands were described as a region with Aboriginal, outdoor recreation, rural lifestyles and paleontological features. The response was very positive and work began on a new tourism destination.

I have been fortunate to contribute to this development. In 2006, I worked with northeast gateway communities to develop their strategic plan for development. This region is not often visited by tourists, even those who live next door. I searched in vain for Calgarians who had visited this part of the province and came away convinced it was like the Empty Quarter, a seldom-visited desert in the Middle East; often mentioned, but never visited.

Christie Dick and Lynette Nelson, from the SAMDA Economic Partnership led the steering committee, and were true superheroes. "Another family is moving away," Christie mentioned over coffee at one meeting. "Is that common?" I asked. "Yes," was the sad reply, "I've kept track of everyone from my high school graduating class; and each year there are fewer of us left."

Christie and Lynette knew how important job creation was in their battle to save their communities and they worked tirelessly to bring their best ideas and best people to the table. We had four committee meetings as we crafted the plan, and as is wont to happen in mid-winter in the prairies, blizzards started during several of the meetings.

Given the size of the region (about half the size of Switzerland), Christie, Lynette, and their group of volunteers were driving up to two hours each way to share their ideas. That they continued to do it in blinding snow reminded me that not just the pony express could be counted on when things must go through.

These daredevils also took time to show us the region's hidden treasures, like tipi rings or mud buttes, often overlooked by tourists. The fact that there were few promotional materials or signs probably accounted for the oversight, after all not all superheroes have x-ray vision. The region has some real gems.

With five thousand people scattered over 20,000 square kilometres, there is lots of land for the deer and the antelope to roam. I was captivated by the landscape, fascinated as the size and numbers of fences declined as I drove from Calgary until finally they petered out all together. Snowy Owls blinked from the occasional telephone pole, and oncoming traffic was so rare, I was able to identify the make and model of each vehicle.

In the years since I finished the strategic plan for the northeast gateway, the Canadian Badlands has continued to evolve. More than 56 municipalities have come together to develop this world-class tourism destination. On their own, they would not survive, but with the leadership of daredevils like Christie and Lynette, they are forging a brighter future. So if you're looking for a vacation idea, help out a daredevil and visit the Canadian Badlands.

Where Everyone Knows Your Name

The Cheers bar may have only existed on a TV show, but many of us search for that place where we are known. It can be even more special when that experience occurs in a foreign country. On a recent visit to Costa Rica, I found the Cheer's equivalent in the Bahia Santa Elena Lodge in the arid Guanacaste Province.

This small, ten-room lodge sits on the main road into a small fishing village nestled next to Santa Rosa National Park. In its previous life, it was a private home. Manuel Allen, a former fisherman, bought the property and painstakingly restored it. The walls of the entire building are covered with wood from the 19th century; I felt like I was nestled in an old sailing ship when I stepped inside.

When the fishing stocks collapsed, Manuel turned his hopes to tourism. If you're holding back at the starting line because you live in a small town and don't think you're powerful enough to make change in the world, you can look to Manuel for inspiration.

Manuel knew that he couldn't count on fishing for his future so he switched to tourism. He opened the lodge and relied on word-of-mouth advertising and his location to generate business. The Lodge is the only accommodation near the National Park and is full most weekends.

The Lodge's rustic flavour appeals to Europeans more than North Americans. Manual thinks Europeans need to save money on lodging after paying more to reach Costa Rica, and the rustic setting seems to appeal to them in general.

I was charmed by the rustic surroundings. The first morning I discovered that everyone in the village takes a shower before the kids go to school and if you want water for the rinse cycle, you should take your shower early. When some of my fellow travelers ran out of water, Manuel turned on his extra pump to fix the problem. When was the last time you had to know what the local routine was before you could take a shower? By being so intimately connected to the community, we had an experience that we wouldn't soon forget and a glimpse into Costa Rican workdays.

So while the Lodge was missing some of the big hotel amenities (a cool swimming pool mid-afternoon would have been nice) there were plenty of compensations. The food, for one. The menus were in Spanish and all the serving staff (including Manuel) spoke only Spanish. My command of the language meant I'd be subsisting on chicken, Coke and cheese unless we found a method to communicate.

Fortunately, Manuel's brother-in-law Ricardo spoke flawless English and translated the menu for us. It took longer than conventional ordering methods, but it was a great icebreaker. "What's that you're eating?" I asked the fellow on my left, "I'm ordering it tomorrow night since it looks so good!"

Without a fancy point-of-sale system or even a computer, the staff took great pains to learn each person's name so they could add your meals and your bar purchases to your account. Hating to feel un-Canadian and unfriendly, I'd ask the staff their names when they called me by name. There were many laughs at the mispronunciation, but genuine bonds were made and it felt like the authentic tourism I often talk about, but seldom find.

Manuel learned our interests as well as our names. A spontaneous whale-watching trip was organized using a local fishing boat. There wasn't a proper pier so passengers were loaded like fireman passing buckets down the brigade, as fishermen passed people from boat to boat. The reward was an afternoon watching a whale and her baby breech as the sun set.

On the final night Manuel and his staff threw a Costa-Rican style barbeque with a local musician. Turns out he was also the gardener, but as so often happens, people have a vocation and an avocation, switching roles as the situation demanded.

Left to my own devices, I would have overlooked the Santa Elena Lodge, yet my visit there was one of the most enjoyable tourism experiences I've had in years. The vision of Manuel Allen has meant jobs when fishing faltered, built esteem in his employees and created bridges between his culture and ours.

Lesson #2

Daredevils Don't Like To
Be Unplugged

Although I'm a daredevil I'm also a desk jockey; researching, writing, forecasting and other things that make me feel mole-like. When I'm not travelling, I ride my horse or explore outdoors for relaxation. I wouldn't consider myself unusually brave in the face of wind, rain and snow, but maybe I am.

Each year it is harder to lure my nephews away from their iPods, Xboxes, computers and cell phones. I have explained warbler identification between their frantic text messaging, and dreamed up new games to deal with the horror of observing Earth Hour with the power off.

I'm not alone in my struggle. We count on technology to do more for us each year and it isn't just for business. These addictive devices help us navigate roads, calculate weight loss progress and record our child's special moments. The convenience makes us reluctant to leave our electrical sources and venture into the outdoors.

I've met many backcountry lodge owners forced to add Internet connections because guests can't be separated from their wireless world, even for a few days. These people may be afraid of losing their jobs and need the combination of technology and wilderness; but will the next generation even visit the backcountry?

In *Last Child in the Woods*, Richard Louv describes the nature-deficit disorder afflicting our children, and how it is leading to obesity, attention disorders and depression. Even if you brush aside these concerns, this disconnect with nature diminishes our ability use the earth's resources wisely.

Research has shown that 1 in 7 Americans think that the ocean is a source of fresh water and a third believe that hydropower is the U.S.'s top power source. Fortunately, daredevils are mobilizing. The No Child Left Behind Coalition has more than 1,600 businesses, health, youth, faith, recreational, environmental and educational groups, representing 50 million people, focusing schools on environmental education.

Other organizations, big and small, are getting into the act with some strategies worthy of any superhero.

Look for Superheroes Under The Bed

I met daredevils Ruth and Warren Clinton when they spoke at a Watchable Wildlife Conference in Rocky Mountain National Park, Colorado. In 1901, Ruth and Warren bought the McGregor Mountain Lodge, and shortly after that, Castle Mountain Lodge, and started a remarkable journey that transformed their community in Colorado.

Estes Park, the community bordering the Rocky Mountain National Park, was struggling with an identity issue in the 1980s. Like many communities, it had cloudy vision when it came to its marketing efforts. The business community debated whether they should promote their stores or their amusement parks and attractions. Ruth had a better idea. "Why don't we focus on the wildlife?" Ruth suggested during one Chamber of Commerce meeting.

Ruth and Warren had seen first hand the power of wildlife to capture people's interest when Bighorn Sheep were reintroduced to the Park. Sheep aren't big readers and didn't get the memo on where they were supposed to live. Instead, they frequented the property surrounding one of the Clinton lodges.

Ruth got used to cars circling her property as people stopped to see the sheep. She also knew they were interested in her other common visitors, the elk.

"Why don't we put an elk on our brochures?" Ruth asked. It might not seem revolutionary now, with wildlife tourism firmly established, but then it was a bold suggestion. The Chamber agreed and they followed up the brochure with information on the best places and ways to watch wildlife. Volunteers directed tourists to safe viewing locations during the rutting season for nature's version of The Bachelor.

The results were unexpected (to some) and rewarding. "We had to double the size of our housekeeping staff," Warren recalls. "Who are people most likely to encounter in a lodge? The housekeepers! We needed to give our staff more training so they could instruct people on how to watch wildlife."

The extra time staff spent on visitor education meant cleaning rooms took longer, but Warren didn't mind. "We now have full occupancy in the fall months, which used to be shoulder months, and we are getting people from further away."

Warren also encountered nature deficit disorder amongst his customers. People weren't content to spend time walking in the woods or rocking on the deck. He offered biking, boating and lots more to provide the variety travelers were seeking. "We also had to teach them to build fires in the fireplaces after we realized people might burn the cabins down if we didn't teach them how!"

Estes Park is now firmly established a premier nature tourism destination, but its origins can be traced to two unlikely superheroes and their team.

Superheroes Ride Horses

The Lone Ranger had Silver, and Calgarian Cathy Thomas has a team of horses as her trusty side-kicks. She uses her equine assistants to teach people about animals. After all, we are animals too, but we don't always recognize our ways have links to the non-human world.

Cathy was the Executive Director of the Calgary Humane Society for many years. She led the organization through a major capital campaign, successfully raising millions for a new building. She also spearheaded several initiatives on responsible pet ownership, but "I started thinking there was a way to do more than 'rescue' animals," Cathy said. "Maybe we could see what animals need and provide that instead of applying a rescue mindset."

She eventually left the Humane Society to explore these possibilities further. An avid horsewoman, she teamed up with Dessa Hockley, the author of *Is Your Horse a Rock Star?,* to promote the book. They knew that a horse's personality affects its performance in the ring, and its relationship with its rider. Their contribution was a personality classification system with easy suggestions for training and activities, like Myers Briggs for horses.

Cathy built on this process with workshops that use horses to teach leadership skills to managers and other professionals. Aptly titled Horseplay, each workshop takes human and horse participants and matches them for team-building and communication exercises.

There is no horse riding in these sessions; instead a group of people work with one horse each to observe how they relate to each other using non-verbal and verbal communication.

"It's amazing," Cathy says, "how much the horses teach us. Initially, I had a detailed lesson plan for the workshops. Then I decided to throw out the formal plan and see how the day evolved. It went better than I expected!"

Cathy supplements her Horseplay workshops with one-on-one coaching and now describes her business activities as "taking care of fifty horses and their families." She helps her clients understand what steps they need to take with their horses and in their lives away from the fields.

She's a daredevil creating new opportunities while building connections between animals and humans. With more like her, we will be more engaged in nature.

Lesson #3

Get Out Of The Phone Booth And Find Other Daredevils

Comic books used to feature one superhero at a time, now they come in Leagues and X-Men type groups. Better things happen when daredevils come together. When I visit a community and find a project proceeding with great fervor and few resources, I know daredevils are at work. With a little investigation, I usually unearth a small group of project champions who are putting their hearts and backbones into the job. These people are adept at getting other people to support the project with money or political clout.

Daredevils build their partnerships by linking their goals with those of possible allies. As every preschooler who cries to get a treat knows, you are more successful if other people have an interest in you getting what you want. Parents want quiet so they give in and provide ice cream or candy. There may be more at stake, but the principles are the same in business, as my next daredevil knows.

Superheroes Help Others Meet Their Goals

"You'll meet your goals if other people want you to meet their goals," Colin Weir wisely says. Another recovering accountant, Colin loves birds and became a falconer at a young age in Ontario. Moving to southern Alberta, he dreamed of his own rescue facility to rehabilitate injured birds of prey and educate people on their value in the ecosystem. "I went to see someone from the tourism department and explained my idea for a wildlife rescue facility that would also become a regional tourism attraction," Colin recalls with a wry laugh, "The fellow said, 'It can't be done! And don't let the door hit you on the way out!"

Colin says, "I thought I might get a better reception with the people from Fish and Wildlife, but I was wrong. They told me "It is illegal for an individual to keep a bird of prey in Alberta. Fortunately, I saw a way to meet my dreams by solving a problem in the community."

The small town of Coaldale suffered from flooding each spring as water flowed over a much-cultivated piece of land and into people's basements. "I told them I could restore the habitat so that the flooding wouldn't be a problem," he said.

"Our owl named Mr. Bogle? He is named for the member of the provincial legislature who believed in our idea," Colin said. With the help of Bob Bogle and then Fish & Wildlife Minister Don Sparrow, who granted special ministerial permission to allow them to hold birds of prey for wildlife rescue, Colin and his co-founder, Wendy Slater, were able to secure land.

Two decades have passed and thousands of birds have been rehabilitated and released back into the wild. In 2005, the facility received funding for a new Interpretative Centre. In 2008, Canadian Geographic awarded Colin's Alberta Birds of Prey Centre a Gold Award for its work in rehabilitation and restoration, validation that Colin's plan to help birds by helping the community was a good idea.

Colin still battles funding challenges, manpower shortages and a sense of urgency as he creates a legacy for future generations. His focus on finding the way forward by helping others has served him well. How could you move forward by helping people overcome their obstacles?

Look for Communities of Superheroes

Think of the changes we can create with partnerships if we find our people, those kindred souls who are working towards the same goals. As Colin Weir discovered, helping other people succeed is a great basis for collaboration. We can also build alliances when we give people a reason to get involved.

I had the privilege one summer, shortly after my dad passed away, of seeing killer whales in the wild. I wasn't prepared for the emotional impact of watching these large creatures slice through the cold, grey waters of Johnstone Straight as they caught breakfast. The whale-watching boat was crowded with people from around the world as excited as I was to see orcas up close.

My enthusiasm quickly turned to horror when our ship interpreter gave us a Canadian history lesson. Orcas were not always seen as a flagship tourism attraction. In fact, marine mammals that had monetary value or threatened commercial fish species have been hunted until very recently.

Between 1913 and 1969 more than 200,000 harbor seals were 'taken' from BC coastal waters because they were considered a nuisance. In the 1960s, fishermen considered bombing killer whales from the air because they believed they were competing for fish stocks. In 1961 in Seymour Narrows, northwest of Campbell River, someone had the unfortunate idea of mounting a Browning machine gun on a boat. The idea was to shoot the dreaded blackfish, as orcas were known, to prevent them from depleting fish stocks. Luckily, the gun was never fired. Afraid that a bullet might ricochet off the water and hurt a person (no such compassion was shown for the poor whales), a government official declared the gun a hazard and it was decommissioned.

I was speechless at hearing this aggression against marine mammals had occurred during my lifetime and in a country with a proud history of national parks and protected areas. What a change forty-five years has

31

brought. A major point this change happened when a researcher named Michael Bigg realized he could identify specific individual orcas by observing their dorsal fins, flukes and color patterns.

This might not seem like the actions of a daredevil, but Dr. Bigg's observations had far-reaching effects. Michael discovered that each whale had unique markings, and by tracking specific animals, researchers could decode their social patterns. The whales were no longer just a group of big fish swimming randomly. We learned they had great intelligence and complex social structures, and we wanted to watch them and protect them.

Enough people cared to stop the attacks and now millions of people a year enjoy whale watching. It has created an industry of whale watching companies, tour guides and conservationists, striving to preserve the whale populations and connect people to marine mammals.

I imagine the people who wanted to shoot whales in decades past would be amazed at the money now paid to watch these amazing creatures. Although I'm still appalled at our earlier treatment of orcas, I am encouraged by the changes in attitude in four short decades. It gives me hope for the bold efforts daredevils are taking to save species, eliminate hunger, stop violence or otherwise improve the world.

But I'm Not Ready To Become a Scientist!

You may not want to go back to school to become a marine biologist and feel exhausted at the idea of changing the world. But I bet you will find your life more engaging if you can find your people, and get involved in activities or discussions about your favorite interests.

My eyes glaze over when people start discussing oil and gas royalty structures, but if someone brings up horse behavior, I get so wrapped up in the discussion, hours pass before I look at my watch. That's what happens when you bond with like-minded daredevils.

Miles Phillips, State Program Leader for Nature Tourism for Texas A&M University's Agrilife Extension Service, shares that belief. I asked Miles to contribute a story for my book, ***Reinventure: How Travel Adventure***

Can Change Your Life. I knew that adventure guides had sparked Miles' shift from environmental engineering to tourism development.

Miles said, "I thought environmental engineering would help me focus on protecting the environment, but I found you are always too late. You are cleaning up messes instead of changing behavior beforehand. So I made a move into nature tourism and guiding."

He suggests people looking for something new find a local interest group. "There are groups for all sorts of interests and if you can find one nearby, it is easy for you to explore your interest and see what else you can do."

I agree with Mile's suggestion. Before a presentation to a naturalists' group, I sat next to a board member. "How did you get involved in this group?" I asked. "My passion is plants," she said, "I volunteer with the rare plants group. It has been fascinating. We spent our last holiday digging up invasive plants so that a rare plant could survive. I've been to some of the most interesting place with my volunteer work. Parks managers take us where help is needed cataloging plants or restoring habitat." Bagging weeds wouldn't be my idea of fun, but this woman glowed as she spoke. She had found her niche and I learned another way to bring a love of plants into a lifestyle.

Albert Teo, my co-author for the book, ***Saving Paradise: The Story of Sukau Rainforest Lodge,*** found a new hobby when looking to generate new business opportunities. "My business needed pictures for marketing brochures and websites. I couldn't afford a professional photographer, so I taught myself photography," he said. It has worked, as his beautiful photographs grace not just his marketing materials, but have been included in several books. Albert also has a hobby that stimulates and provides hours of enjoyment.

So, next time you find yourself feeling like life is more of the same old, same old, think about broadening your horizons. Is there an interest you would like to explore or a cause you could throw your weight behind? Chances are, there is a group of other daredevils waiting to meet you!

Lesson #4

Choosing the Right Costume

Superman's blue tights and red shorts are a look most of us can't carry off, and that is a good thing. But I have to admire him for pushing the envelope, and picking something streamlined that capitalized on his ability to fly.

Many organizations I encounter are not as quick to identify their strengths and capitalize on them. Instead of shopping in the red spandex section, they go right to basic black wool. There is a dearth of venues to foster business creativity and innovation, unless you count the inebriated ramblings at the company's summer barbeque.

Globalization puts greater emphasis on efficiency. Most people are so focused on meeting deadlines, coming up with new ways of doing something seems too risky; failure to implement could implode their carefully-balanced world.

But there are daredevils who are taking risks and breaking from tradition. They are taking established processes and turning them upside down. The results are exciting. New income sources from activities you might dismiss as impractical. Employees excited about the changes in their workplace. Not all of them apply to your life or organization, but the way these daredevils have innovated has lessons for us all.

Can Riding the Bus Change Your Life?

Can riding the bus change your life? That's not the kind of slogan used by Calgary Transit, but is could be if it wants to change. One of my most-admired people is Keith Miles, a transplanted Newfoundlander I worked with at Dome Petroleum many years ago. Now Keith owns a successful software company and spends his winter traveling Southeast Asia.

What makes Keith's travel so remarkable is that he runs his company and makes money while on the road. This is unlike most of us who spend money while traveling.

Keith sets up shop in the world's most beautiful hotels; and through the use of a data stick, Skype and remote meeting software, carries on business across the globe. His wife, Gerry, left her nursing job to help Keith. With them both working on the family business, they are able to explore to their heart's content.

"We need to stay in a major centre for two weeks each month," Keith explains, "I need reliable Internet for my month end processes. But once those routines have been run, we can travel to the remote areas and really enjoy ourselves." Not that staying at Bangkok's legendary Shangri-La Hotel is any kind of hardship. Its lush gardens along the Chao Phraya River provide a stunning backdrop for a remote office.

Keith arrived at this remarkable place by reading a book while riding the C-Train. Obviously, it wasn't just any book. Frustrated with delays in getting new reports from accounting software, Keith took a step that most of us don't.

Instead of shrugging off the countless postponements associated with software development, Keith took matters into his own hands. He bought a book on Access databases and read it while commuting. "I figured I could do that (write reports) so I taught myself Access while riding the C-Train," he said.

Soon Keith was writing the reports he needed, but he didn't stop there. He created a series of software programs for joint venture administration.

Sometimes he 'mines' data, looking for unbilled service fees, paying his fees several times over from the recovered monies.

Keith discovered that if he could meet his clients' needs from his home office, he could move his office wherever he had Internet access. That is how he came to be doing monthly accounting in Sydney, Australia; Bangkok and other vacation destinations. What are you doing with your commuting time?

Does it Take a Superhero to Make Money in the Arts?

What if your organization or your career interests revolve around visual or performing arts? You may think it is area where it is difficult to make money, but it doesn't have to be that way. With some creativity in your business model and some drive, you can turn it into a moneymaker.

Roger and Keri Duncan of One World Drum created a drumming community in Calgary's oil and gas culture by turning customers into tribal members. I remember signing up for a drumming workshop with One World Drum. They promised anyone could make music and I was going to put them to the test. My musical history was limited to painful attempts to play the recorder in Grade Four.

As we sat in the slightly dusty high school utility room, Roger taught us the basic sounds of the drum. He also taught us something more important, that you only need one really good drummer to sound great.

"You'll be doing this song in your recital," he said at the end of the class. "What recital?" my inner voice screamed. There had been no mention of a performance in the brochure. I hadn't planned a public demonstration of my neophyte drumming skills, but One World Drum had other ideas.

When the shock wore off, my classmates and I realized Roger would be dragging us in front of a live audience six weeks hence. We hung onto his every instructional word for the next five classes. I practiced drumming on my dining room table and the clothes dryer.

All too soon, the big night arrived. 'Performers' got free admission, but friends and family had to pay a cover charge. I noticed they didn't offer refunds so I hoped no one would be disappointed. The One World Drum staff was selling drinks and snacks. I figured a tipsy new drummer would sound worse than a sober new drummer and ordered a Coke.

"It's time to get on the stage," Roger told us. Approaching the stage with the dread dieters show when led to the weigh scale, we settled into our chairs with our drums.

"Remember to breathe," Roger said, knowing we would hold our breath until our nerves passed. I expected most of us to turn blue. He turned to the crowd and started the drumming, cueing us to start our lines. I was surprised at how good we sounded for beginners, and the audience seemed to enjoy the music. I was grateful no one ran for the exits.

I learned from this experience that the music would come if we supported each other, and I appreciated the business model One World Drum had created. By giving every student an immediate goal, in my case it was avoiding public humiliation, they created a need for more drumming lessons. They also created a revenue stream at the recitals as each student brought, or dragged, friends and family to be in the audience.

I got tired of practicing on flat surfaces and bought a drum from One World Drumming as did many of the students. If the recitals got routine, One World Drum had a performing group more experienced drummers could join. All of these activities have created a lifestyle supported by music.

Take Your Leotards Dancing

Another person who has found a way to combine her love of art with making a living is Sue Hall of New Attitude Line Dancing. Sue discovered her passion after taking a line dancing class. "I was horrible at it," she said of her first class. She obviously overcame those early missteps as she now leads her dance company and classes with grace and finesse.

Some might describe Sue's business as dance instruction, but it is much more. Line dancing is great exercise, balancing mind and body. It attracts lots of people for fitness, but much of its charm lies in the fact that you don't need a partner. If my husband is any indication, more women than men like dancing, so line dance is a great way to shake your boots and bootie without shaking your relationship.

Sue's innovative business model builds a community as well as dancing skills. In addition to lessons, Sue holds dance evenings with snacks and socializing, plus the chance to learn new routines.

For several years, the New Attitude Line Dancers performed during the Calgary Stampede. I performed one year, and I can attest to the extra dedication it brought to my craft. I practiced our routines wherever there was enough ground to link ten steps together which, much to husband's horror, included our front deck.

Line dancing becomes more than a hobby for those involved. You can go to line dancing conventions, learning new dances and dressing up for theme nights. Sue also organizes cruise vacations for line dancers, a great chance to kick up your heels and see the sights.

Some of Sue's students dance through medical treatments or use it as a distraction from family troubles. Sue uses her student community to raise awareness for people needing assistance; and, in 2007, started Teen Angels Calgary, a charity providing Christmas gifts to disadvantaged teen-agers. Many of her dancers donate gifts or money, showing that dancing can make the world go round.

Chasing Cattle Pays

I've never met the entrepreneur who aims for poor customer service, although I've certainly experienced plenty. Most people say they focus on customers, but do they really?

I think many businesses provide what they think the client should want, not what the marketplace is seeking. Never have I seen this more clearly demonstrated than when visiting Costa Rica.

As part of a Texas A&M University Extension agritourism tour, we did a cattle drive. This was a short cattle drive, two hours long, not the two days or more that cowboys usually spend.

The group showed up at the cattle drive launch with scuffed riding boots and jeans; most of the people had riding experience, but that didn't seem important to the local wranglers. They spoke Spanish, not English, so there was no talk about riding experience or rules.

We were given a helmet to don, a waiver to sign, and a horse to mount. The horses were shorter and skinnier than the quarter horses we were used to, and so were the saddles!

There was no orientation on how to herd cows, or even the cowboys' names. Our horses pulled on the reins and jockeyed for position; they didn't run nose to tail like seen in on western trail rides. Instead we bounced two and three abreast down the trail until we came to the cattle.

There was no order to our 'drive'. With no instructions, we deduced that it might be better to follow the staff and mimic their moves which consisted of a lot of hand waving and yelling 'OH! OH! "I have found a Spanish word I can pronounce without an accent," I thought gleefully.

My horse liked being eyeball to eyeball with the cows; an experienced cow horse, I thought. Little did I know how experienced she was.

With minimal fuss, we herded the cows back down the road to the paddock. Aside from the fact we brought a bull back with the cows, it was a huge success. We were congratulating ourselves on a job well done, when I noticed another group of riders gearing up. They mounted the horses we had just ridden, the cowboys opened the gates, and they proceeded to chase the cows down the road.

By now, I had a theory. We met the Ranch manager to learn more about his operation. "Are those people taking the cows back to where we found them?" I asked. "Yes," he said. "Will there be another group after them driving the cows back to the paddock?" I queried. "Yes," he said. "So, basically, you have one group after another moving those cows to the pasture and back again?" I asked. When he replied in the affirmative, the ranchers in our group were outraged. "You can't do that," one said, "The meat off those cows will be as tough as shoe-leather."

"How has your business been? Have you been hurt by the recession?" I asked. "What recession?" the manager said with a chuckle, "I have about 6,000 tourists a month come to my ranch." Many of the businesses we had seen had decreases of twenty or thirty percent from the recession, but this fellow was not only weathering the economic downturn, he was thriving. "It appears there is more money to be made chasing cows, than raising cows," I said to our group.

I thought of all the cow-calf operators I know who struggle, yet going on a cattle drive at western ranches is hard to do. The ranchers take the cows to pasture in May, brand them mid-summer, and bring them back in late fall. If your schedule doesn't match that of the ranch, there will be no cattle drive for you. How many people would be happy and would pay to move cattle, even if it isn't when the cattle need to move?

The Costa Rican rancher had turned his cattle from food stock to part of the staff, paid entertainers, if you will. They were used to being herded by amateurs, and they generated a lot of income for their efforts. How many businesses overlook a chance for better customer service and more revenue because that they are stuck on the way it's always been done?

Lesson #5

Not so Fast, Lone Ranger

Tonto got second billing to the Lone Ranger, but things are changing. One in twenty-five Canadians are Aboriginal, and Canada's Aboriginal population is the fastest growing in the country. More than half of Aboriginals live in urban areas, meaning they are almost as likely to live in the city as you.

The Aboriginal population is younger, on average, than the rest of the population. With an expected labor shortage when baby boomers retire, business leaders may turn to this group for solutions. Unfortunately, there are big gaps in Aboriginal education levels and social conditions.

People will be paying more attention to Aboriginal affairs as the years unfold. Not only are Aboriginal youth a possible solution for labor shortages, there more than 1,000 unsettled land claims. The cost of settling these claims will be considerable, and since most disputed lands cannot be returned in their original form, we will see new partnerships between Aboriginals and non-Aboriginals.

Carol Patterson

Ancient Superheroes

Long before Batman donned his cape, there were men avenging wrongs and fighting for their people. The Haida nation on British Columbia's northern coast is well known for their ocean-going canoes. The Haida were also fierce warriors, and skeptical when they contacted white explorers.

They would toss the colored beads they were offered on the beach, refusing to trade their valuable pelts for baubles. The Haida enjoyed a rich diet, growing tall and strong. Their superhero stature intimidated the Europeans. Unfortunately, the Haida were no match for Smallpox and other diseases brought by the Europeans. Their populations were decimated and survivors gathered on the north island of Haida Gwaii.

In time, logging started in Haida Gwaii, known at the time as the Queen Charlotte Islands. The large trees of the old-growth forests were much favored by the forestry companies, and one can still see the scars from aggressive clear-cutting. In 1974, in response to Haida protests, Premier Dave Barrett promised logging would stop on traditional food gathering areas. There was a deferral, but not a permanent moratorium.

As logging continued, Haida activists including Giindajin Haawasti Guujaaw took the government to court. Even though jobs were needed, Guujaaw and other Haida felt preservation of the trees was more important.

The Haida joined forces with environmentalists to save the islands. They were successful. In 1985, the Haida Nation designated Gwaii Hannas a Haida Heritage site, and in 1987 logging stopped with the signing of South Moresby Memorandum of Understanding with Canadian and British Columbia governments.

This agreement led to the establishment of Gwaii Hannas National Park, and is proof that a daredevil attitude is needed for bold changes.

In 1993, the Gwaii Hannas Agreement was signed, establishing common objectives for the Park's protection. It also provides for a unique power sharing arrangement between the Haida and Parks Canada.

I was able to visit Gwaii Hannas National Park and found the experience different from other parks. Haida Watchmen reside at five heritage sites. Traditionally, Watchmen guarded Haida settlements, warning the chief when danger was approaching. Now Watchmen mind the cultural history of their people.

Although most of the sites' structures are returning to the earth and look like ruins to non-Aboriginals, the Haida regard these sacred places as a living part of its culture. Although our Parks Managers might normally restore some of these structures, the Haida want them to return to the earth, as they feel is natural. To keep the experience on the Haida sites special, only twelve visitors can visit at one time. Tourists are greeted on the beach by a Watchman who leads a tour of the site and shares some history.

When visiting T'aanuu Llnagaay (Tanu), I met Watchman Sean Young, a knowledgeable and engaging representative of the Haida culture. The trails are marked with neat rows of clamshells, ensuring we stayed to the trails. We were also told not to sit on any logs lying on the ground. It's possible these logs were fallen memorial polls, and sitting on them would be hugely disrespectful, like putting your bottom on the church altar.

"I checked with my uncle and he said it would be okay if you stepped off the path to see what I want to show you," Sean said. "Parks Canada would normally tell you to stay on the paths, but this park is co-managed between Parks Canada and our people, so I can go to my uncle for his direction.

"My uncle and I discuss what I want to do, and then he will ask me what I think would be best," Sean explained. The next three hours flew by as we learned more. Sean was engaging, and had us laughing as he provided insight to his culture. "Haida people have always been tall and strong yet I've seen the biggest Haida reduced to silence by their aunties. We are matrilineal with power passing through our mother's side of the family," he explained.

With a laugh, he continued, "My mother told me she brought me into this world, and she could take me out!" Women's rights were firmly established with this culture long before the west coined 'women's liberation'.

During my time on Haida Gwaii, I learned that the Haida have a much longer planning horizon than western cultures. They would manage a forest, watching for decades over specific trees that would eventually be suitable for canoes. How many times have I seen someone standing impatiently in front of a microwave because it isn't fast enough? Our emphasis on efficiency, speed and profit bodes poorly for our future.

Hopefully we can adapt some of the Haida lessons in long term planning to the problems facing our world.

Are Superhero Qualities Inherited?

Where I live, there are many Aboriginal groups; my hometown is located on land that was Blackfoot territory. The Blackfoot Confederacy includes the Peigan, Kainai and the Siksika. Their life was based upon hunting buffalo and when the buffalo were hunted to extinction, times got tough for the Blackfoot.

Their leaders believed that signing a treaty with the Europeans was necessary to survive, and negotiations started between the government and Chief Crowfoot. Chief Crowfoot was a wise leader and believed that peaceful relations with the government were necessary for cultural and spiritual survival.

In 1877, he signed Treaty 7 and his people settled on reserves. This was a great hardship as his people adapted to a new way of life. Eventually they learned to farm and ranch, although other problems challenged the Blackfoot, including the disruption to their social fabric by residential schools.

Now they are preserving their culture and telling the world their stories. On the site where Treaty 7 was signed, the world-class Blackfoot Crossing Historical Park has risen. I worked with the Blackfoot to expand their skills in programming and customer service, but I think the Blackfoot taught me as much as I taught them.

They shared stories of their upbringing on the reserve, and spiritual events seldom talked about with outsiders. I don't feel I can share these stories as they are the Blackfoot's to tell. However, I was struck by one conversation I had with an elder.

"The ancestors said that there would come a generation that would be smarter than anybody," he said. "Look at these young men," he said, pointing to the facility's leaders. "Aren't they bright and capable young people? Our future looks very good with these people leading." I agreed.

So was it foresight of the ancestors? Can you tell when the next generation of superheroes or daredevils will show up? Most people would say not, but I often think back to that conversation, and admire the First Nations for their prophetic abilities and their faith in them. We could do well to do the same.

Lesson #6

Corporations Nurture Daredevils

Most of us can't leap a pile of dirty laundry, never mind a building. So wouldn't it be nice to have someone with real might help you reach your goals? If you're lucky, you work with a company that has a superhero attitude, one that nurtures daredevils.

In this day and age, corporations are looking beyond debits and credits. To retain quality employees, they need engaged employees and good community relations for long-term success. This has meant more organizations are embracing social responsibility and community involvement.

Working for a daredevil organization can make your work more fulfilling. Don't you feel a sense of pride when your employer helps the less fortunate or your favorite charity? How about when they encourage you to live your best life by learning new skills or taking time for family?

I don't work for a large corporation, but I come across many daredevil employers. I think their commitment to social responsibility makes for happier employees, supports clients and builds great communities in which to live and work. I like to give my business to these companies as well.

Under That Banker's Suit Lurks a Superhero

I'm a long time bank customer of RBC. They take great care of my money and me. I love the personal service I get each time I call Sam. He's technically my financial planner, but he also doubles as the person who answers all questions related to banking. I know I can phone Sam with the most unusual requests (and trust me, self-employed tourism consultants have some weird ones) and he tackles each one with know-how and good humor. He's a superhero to me, and he works for an organization that helps many other people.

RBC is part of this growing corporate movement that supports community causes in innovative ways. I remember the first time I stopped to make a bank deposit and saw everyone wearing bright T-shirts advocating an end to homelessness. It looked like they were preparing for a night on the streets (and I think some were), but they were contributing money and time to solve a very visible problem in my city. It turns out my bank is leading Canadian banks in corporate responsibility rankings and that's a nice feeling. I almost feel happy about the service fees I pay!

One organization, especially a large one, can make a big difference with its social actions. The RBC invested $105 million in donations and sponsorships in 2009. That is a lot of community support! Even Superman would be impressed.

RBC makes giving personal as well. Employees who volunteer more than 40 hours receive $500 for their charity. When I was logging 40 hours a month as a Calgary Zoo volunteer, I would have appreciated this support. Maybe I would have felt I could change the world, without changing employers!

The Wind Beneath Your Wings

There is a love song with the words "the wind beneath my wings", but corporations can fill this role, literally. The Alberta Birds of Prey Centre I mentioned in Lesson 3 has an ongoing partnership with Fortis Inc., a large utility company. In 2008, the FortisAlberta Flying Field was constructed to provide a demonstration theatre for education programs.

The field includes a non-energized power line display. Obviously, fricasseeing a bird during a flying demo would be a showstopper, so the display seems like an obvious safety feature, but it goes beyond that. Fortis is committed to reducing the electricity dangers to birdlife, not just at the Centre, but in the fields and roadways around the country. They want to show people that Fortis is taking steps to protect birds. A win-win for everyone!

Don't Mess Around With Your Cape, Just Do It

Nike says "just do it" in their advertising campaigns and CBC Calgary, a public radio station, has adapted the motto, creating the Do Crew. When I first heard the name, I thought it was the Dew Club and they were focused on gardening!

The Do Crew doesn't garden, but they tackle almost everything else. It is a loosely organized volunteer group of CBC staff and listeners who help a different organization every few weeks on a specific job. During the Calgary Stampede they were building a float with the YWCA to celebrate that organization's 100th anniversary.

The Do Crew also built a meditation labyrinth using duct tape for Wellspring Calgary, a cancer support organization. It would seem to be a sticky project, but one with lots of rewards. Angela Knight and Michael Arnault, two of CBC's colorful personalities, spearhead the Do Crew.

Angela is strongly committed to community and staying connected. "I make sure we're out there, actively talking to people on their own terms, on their own turf," says Angela. She certainly walks the talk. Angela and Michael and their 400 do-gooders have logged more than 1,400 volunteer hours in little more than a year. Not only does the time donated help the causes they select, the exposure on Calgary's number-one-rated morning program doesn't hurt either. Spiderman would be impressed.

Going to the Birds

Sometimes corporations take a more active role in a community organization. On the central Alberta farm of Charlie and Winnie Ellis, you can find the highest concentration of nesting mountain bluebirds ever recorded in their range. This concentration came from Charlie and Winnie's superhuman efforts to build birdhouses and suitable habitat.

When they could no longer manage their farm and the bluebird houses in the 1970s, Charlie and Winnie found a partner who could preserve their legacy. Union Carbide was looking for a location for their ethylene glycol facility and the Ellis farm was ideally situated.

Charlie and Winnie sold the farm on the proviso that the company would look after the birds. And look after the birds they have. An arm's length, non-profit company was established in 1982 to look after the birds and the homestead where a visitor centre now sits. A volunteer board governs with representatives from the Red Deer Naturalists, the Federation of Alberta Naturalists, MEGlobal Canada Inc. (the current owners of the facility), the County of Lacombe and community members.

The bluebirds continue to raise their young on the Ellis farm and each year about 6,000 people come to see the birds and learn about habitats and bird-friendly gardens. MEGlobal Canada continues a successful operation next door and is proof that corporate and environmental interests can merge.

Lesson #7

Daredevils Come in All Sizes and Ages

You may think you can't be a daredevil because you're too old or too young or too shy or too whatever. Excuses like daredevils, come in all sizes and shapes. But that is just what they are – excuses, not reasons to stay in a rut.

Many times excuses cover-up the fear of leaving our comfort zone. That is normal. If you don't feel fear, chances are you aren't trying something new or challenging. I'm not advocating the knee-knocking fear Evel Knievel's jumps would create for most of us. I'm suggesting that if your heart isn't thumping or your stomach fluttering from time to time, you are probably stuck to the safe and narrow at the expense of new experiences.

I spend time on the straight and narrow and it's comfortable; but if you never leave your normal routine you are probably missing some of life's great moments. It is hard, but I'm learning to accept fear. I can't count the number of times I've found myself in a situation that has me saying "I'm never doing this again!" only to find myself months later, doing something very similar or scarier. My explanation for such strange behavior is that once the fear passes, I enjoy what I'm doing, or take pride in having tackled something new.

I won't ever be as brave as Spiderman scaling buildings, but I'm working on making fear a friend. I don't think we'll ever be best friends, but I know when fear shows up, I've got a chance to feel more intensely. Often this leads to new friends and new stories.

So let's see what we can accomplish when we put the excuses aside and take small steps into the unknown.

Learn From Children

Spirit, a golden eagle, came to know people when she was shot several times. Fortunately, someone who knew about the Alberta Birds of Prey Centre in Southern Alberta found her. They put the eagle in their minivan, strapping her in the back seat like an odd-shaped child, and drove to the facility.

Volunteers nursed Spirit back to health, although the bullets damaged her eyes and she never regained her sight. Since she is blind, she cannot be released to the wild. Instead she has become an amazing ambassador for her species and the Center.

Of the many people inspired by Spirit's story are two nine-year-old girls, Sierra Tanner and Madison Strombecky. They rallied their classmates to action, raising money for Spirit's long-term care. Sierra and Madison made presentations to groups like the Banff Ski Club and even the Calgary Petroleum Club. In a few months, they raised over $15,000!

More people are getting involved as a result of Sierra and Madison's efforts. Paul Rasporich at Calgary Arts Academy encouraged his students to write a song about Spirit. Their efforts, along with the help of instructor Cam Bourque, caught the eye of legendary singer Ian Tyson. Talks are now underway to make a recording with Ian Tyson and the students at Calgary Arts Academy.

Great things can happen from meeting wild creatures! And, as Colin Weir, founder of the Birds of Prey Centre says, "We now know that if we want something done, we need to turn it over to two nine-year olds!"

A Cheesy Story: Don Carlos Farm

"I knew if I could get the best restaurants to buy from me, the other restaurants and hotels would follow!" enthused Rodolfo Vargas Blanco, one of the founders of Don Carlos Farm in La Fortuna, Costa Rica. I was participating in the Texas A & M University's tour of innovative nature and agritourism businesses. This was our second stop of the day, but we were hearing some of the most interesting revelations of the week.

Rodolfo is younger than you might expect when you arrive at the entrance such a large farm, but there is no missing his enthusiasm. As he described how Don Carlos Farm tours got started, his words flowed faster until I expected to see him vibrate out of his shoes. Obviously, tourism and farming were subjects close to his heart.

"My father is Don Carlos, and he started this farm many years ago," Rodolfo explained. "It is one of the largest dairy farms in the area with 400 cows. Six years ago, the dairy company who buys our milk told all the farmers in the area to expand, as they would buy as much milk as we could produce. Then when we had gone into debt and expanded, they said they couldn't buy the milk. It almost broke us. Many farmers did go broke."

Rodolfo had been encouraged to follow his own path by his parents and was an economics student when these events unfolded. Putting his university education to practical use, he worked with his family on ideas to save the family farm.

Their best bet was making cheese from their milk and selling it restaurants and stores, so Rodolfo used his education to his benefit. "Every school project became research for the farm. I did a survey of local chefs as a school project to find out what they wanted. The label for the cheese was even designed during a school project."

Rodolfo, wise beyond his years, waited until he had done his research before he created a product. His knowledge of what the market desired resulted in a cheese sought after by the top chefs in the region.

What I found most interesting was how the farm came to be a tourism attraction. Rodolfo recalled the story of when he had signed up for a cheese farm tour several years earlier. Brimming with excitement, he arrived for the tour. "I had tons of paper and was ready to write down cheese recipes and every detail I could absorb," he recalled.

The tour wasn't what he expected. Rodolfo saw the cheese manufacturing, briefly, through a small window. There was no mention of recipes and no time to discuss cheese nuances. Instead, "They took us to the offices and showed us around the accounting department and the other departments. There wasn't much to learn about cheese, but I remember they had some pretty secretaries," he said with a laugh.

However, the trip wasn't a total failure. With an entrepreneur's eye, he looked at all the people gathered for the $20 cheese peep show and walk-through of an office building, and asked how popular the tours were. "250,000 people come each year," was the reply. He almost fell over in shock! "That is a lot of money," he thought. And that was when he decided he had a future in tourism.

The Don Carlos Farm now offers wagon tours through the fields and surrounding forest, a chance to milk a cow, and visit a restaurant and cheese shop. You can stop to enjoy a guided tour or bike through the farm to get an up-close look at the farming lifestyle. "People really like the idea that they are saving the environment and the land by visiting the farm," Rodolfo says.

One of the other Vargas brothers will build cottages so guests can stay overnight and experience more rural life. So the family has been successful where others have failed by combining good business practices with innovation and being brave enough to let the younger generation lead in difficult circumstances. Not for the faint of heart, but farmers were in the risk business long before tourism came along.

The Courage to Tackle Monkey Business

Change in our lives often comes when things are uncomfortable or when we are at our lowest. As I mentioned, I made the decision to go back to school partly because my work situation had become very unpleasant. If I had been enjoying my workdays, it's unlikely I would have become a mature student and forgone the comfort of a regular paycheque.

You may find the same thing. When your life has few complaints, you will continue doing what you've been doing for months or years. But then something happens. Your spouse becomes unemployed or your kids leave home (or you wish they would). Sometimes it is just waking up one morning to a life that has gotten so predictable you wonder if this is all there is.

As rough at that might feel, it can be a great time to add new activities to your life. You may have ideas as to what those might be, but you may be afraid to make the change. You might encounter resistance from those closest to you. Or you might find the resistance comes from within.

Elizabeth Scott encountered resistance and fear when she decided in mid-life to study anthropology. She was fascinated by primates and wanted to understand their world. She discovered a field study program for Snow Monkeys in southern Texas. How Snow Monkeys came to be in southern Texas is a story for another day, but how Elizabeth came to be in southern Texas has lessons for us all.

When she told her husband she wanted to take the class, he said, "Why would you want to do that?" Elizabeth had her own doubts. "I was the oldest person in the class," she recalls, "I was afraid to do what I really wanted, so I committed in steps. I put my name down for the class thinking I wouldn't be selected. Then when I was selected, I decided I would make up my mind when it was time to book my flight. Then when it was time to book my flight, I told myself I had time to cancel."

Moving towards her goal with small steps and allowing herself an escape hatch took some of the pressure off Elizabeth and helped her move towards her goal. If she had needed to make the full leap without the support of family, it might have been too big and she may have missed the field school.

As it was, Elizabeth loved her time studying the monkeys. Her experience was different than some of the younger students; she was focused on her time with the monkeys and wasn't interested in the socializing of the younger students.

"I would find myself at the camp with few other people around and we had the most amazing encounters with the monkeys," she recalls. "I am so glad I overcame the resistance that was holding me back. My mother, who wasn't exactly supportive at the time, now has Alzheimer's. So if I had stayed home because of her disapproval, it would have been for nothing, as she doesn't remember now."

Learn to Work With Fear

"You'll know when you get to the first section if you want to do it; it only gets uglier from there," said the young woman, wiping sweat from her brow. She had just finished descending Picacho Peak and I was eager for more details. Arizona State Parks described the Picacho Peak climb as a difficult hike, saying gloves were a must for the cables on the final scramble the 1500-foot climb. Cables? Scrambling?! Most of my hiking requires little more than good boots and a good lunch. Pulling myself along cables and dangling over the desert floor sounded entirely too strenuous for a relaxing holiday afternoon, but the trip would provide a great life lesson on overcoming fear and removing labels that limit us.

The first hikers we met on the scenic Sunset Vista trail approach recommended we tackle the upper portion. "You should do it at least once," they echoed, sounding a bit like college students encouraging you to try tequila shooters and forgetting all about the subsequent fallout. I noticed the women in the group were unusually quiet and didn't seem to share the enthusiasm of their male counterparts.

Whenever someone waxed poetic about the climb they seemed to avoid eye contact; I should have recognized that for the foreboding that it was.

"You'll be fine," one fellow said in parting, "as long as you don't have a fear of heights." I do. Or perhaps I should say I did.

As we picked away at the two-mile approach I wasn't sure if I should tackle the peak. The hike sounded intriguing and my husband Colin loves ambitious hikes. Weighing against this was my fear of heights. Deciding this was a good time to develop some mental toughness, I resolved not to decide (panic) until I reached the first set of cables. Once I saw the trail, I would know if I had the skills or the motivation. Or if got really lucky, it would start to rain and the decision would be taken out my hands!

A good hiker never overlooks lunch; at the end of the Sunset Vista trail we found a rock perch and assessed the trail ahead. Using binoculars, I spotted hikers pulling themselves along the cables. I could almost see them grimacing. "Looks tough," I thought, mentally planning a relaxing afternoon at camp once I turned back.

So how did I find myself undertaking a hike harder than one I had ever done? The first set of cables was not as scary as expected. The cables went straight up a vertical rock face about fifty feet, but rock walls sheltered both sides. It looked like an indoor climbing wall with a great view. Since I had tried climbing walls and liked it, I decided to give the first section a go. I could assess my options after my Spiderman imitation; if they were bad, I would turn around and say sanity had returned.

There were many small grooves in the rock so finding footholds was not hard. The breathing was harder; this was work I was not used to. I stopped halfway to suck extra air and to put my lungs back in my chest! I resolved to add extra pushups to my daily fitness routine.

When I eventually crawled onto the first ledge, I was surprised at how well I had done. "Let's keep going," I told Colin. He would not have been more surprised if I had told him I wanted season's hockey tickets. We came across a couple more cable sections, some of them so narrow they tangled with my pack and hiking poles, making me feel like a spider caught in a web. The view down was scary in places and a reminder to pay attention if I didn't want to skydive without the airplane. I chose instead to look up and leave the sightseeing for later.

When I was started to falter, I caught sight of another hiker a few metres ahead. He had grey hair and was carrying a water bottle in one hand as he balanced off the cable. My water bottle was safely in my pack, as I needed two hands, two feet and some crazy glue to keep from falling. I am probably guilty of ageism, but I thought if this fellow is doing it, I could too! Before long we had caught up to him and exchanged pleasantries.

Max explained that he was hiking on his own although his sons had warned him not to climb the peak or to hike alone. Enjoying his company, we continued our climb with Max, figuring we could minimize his risk by hiking with him although there was no doubt we were all headed to the top. In a joking aside to Colin, I asked, "When did we go from corrupting our nephews with adventure trips to corrupting other people's parents?"

After seventy-five minutes we had finished our 1,500-foot climb and were standing on the summit of Picacho Peak. Located approximately half way between Tucson and Phoenix I could see the smog of Phoenix to the north and the Santa Rosa Mountains to the southwest. It was beautiful, but I didn't spend time wallowing in triumph. Going down would be harder than going up. And there were no escalators to make the cable sections easier.

The descent got tough in a hurry. The cautious approach meant I was backing down the mountain like one would go down a ladder. Unlike a ladder there were no regularly spaced steps. In some places there didn't appear to be any steps at all. "Who moved them?" I thought; I had found them on the way up. Colin saved the day, going ahead to place my feet in safer spots to avoid becoming a young widower. In places where there were no footholds I could reach, he used his foot as a brace for mine.

Although I was afraid of ending up on the evening news under the headline "Helicopter needed to rescue hiker off Picacho Peak", I made it down without putting a claim on my travel insurance. As I reached the last cable I was doing a jig that could land me a spot on America's Got Talent!

As we hiked to the trailhead, I mulled over the adventure. I hated being stuck without footholds, but clinging to the mountain was not as frightening as I had anticipated. Was it time to remove the label 'a person afraid of heights'? I think so. I would even do it again, perhaps after time smoothed the rough edges from this vacation memory. Once more I was convinced that learning to keep going even in the face of fear was worth it. Too many things are left undone and untried if we stop every time we feel fear.

Strength of Mind

As I found on Picacho Peak, if we can quiet our minds' incessant chatter of what cannot be done or should be done, we may find that our fear or resistance goes away. On a sailing trip to Haida Gwaii, I was impressed with fellow passenger Stephanie Fowler's sailing knowledge. "Have you always been a keen sailor?" I asked. I figured someone who knew so much about the winds and sailing vernacular had been born with a love of sailing. I was only partially right. Although she loves sailing now, it wasn't always that way.

"I hated to sail when I was younger," she said. "My parents loved to sail but I was afraid of the noise and the movement of the boat. When I was twelve I went away to summer camp and it was an odd camp. I remember my parents coming to visit and me begging them to take me with them. They were in the middle of a sailing trip so they said they would take me out of the camp to go sailing with them, but if I was going to come I had to like sailing. They didn't want me sulking or being afraid. I had to like it! And I did. From that point on, I liked sailing."

Stephanie's transformation from sailing hater to enthusiast proves that changing our minds is often the biggest change needed for success.

So to keep your journey on track, surround yourself with positive people. Avoid those people who 'should' all over you. You know whom I mean. The people who say, "You should like what I like", or "You should do this."

Sometimes avoiding the 'shoulds' is hard because they come from within. Another passenger on the sailing trip was telling me of her son who wanted to be a marine biologist. He decided there were no jobs for marine biologists so he took engineering instead. "I told him not to worry about whether there are jobs. He should do what he loved, she said. "Now he is almost finished his PhD in Engineering and there are tons of jobs in marine biology. He doesn't know what to do now." I wonder if he thinks about what life would be like if he had ignored the fear and studied marine biology.

Lesson #8

We Need Superhero Policies

I meet a lot of superheroes in my work. They are battling overwhelming obstacles like someone is trotting around a chunk of kryptonite, trying to scare them off their tasks.

Not only is it much easier when there are other superheroes to share the load as we discussed earlier, it is even easier if everyone is guided by superhero policies. I never gave much thought to policies when I started my business. I thought they were no more than a bunch of long words strung together by lawyers and government officials. It felt at times like their purpose was to get in the way of actually accomplishing something.

I'm older and wiser now, and I realize that good policies can shape the way the world looks. Look at litter. Governments in Canada have a policy requiring drink vendors to charge a refundable deposit. By putting a price on the head of each can, they have ensured that people will return their empty cans. Or if people are super villains and toss their can into the ditch, some enterprising soul will come along and rescue it because it is worth money.

Superheroes from Different Worlds

Our world needs more superhero policies, especially when it comes to the environment. Many governments talk about sustainability as a worthwhile goal, but lack the legislation and policies to make it happen.

Bhutan, a country in the Himalayan Mountains, showed me how daredevils can shape innovative policies in the face of conventional wisdom, and come up with better solutions to the world's problems.

When I told people I was off to Bhutan, most of them answered with "Where's that?" Some even asked, "What's that?" Obviously, Bhutan is off the daredevil map, at least for some people.

People don't know about Bhutan because it is one of the world's least visited countries with around 20,000 annual visitors. Consider that Nepal gets that many tourists in two weeks, and you start to understand how undiscovered this place is.

When people ask me what country I'm from, I get impressed reactions when I say I'm from Canada. We pride ourselves on our friendliness and peaceful status. I wonder what if feels like to be Bhutanese where few have heard of your country.

Bhutan obscurity is due to its government policies around tourism and development. The Bhutanese are Buddhist and its leaders take a long term, daredevil approach to growth.

Tourists were not allowed in the country until 1974; even then the first tourists were guests of the king, not busloads of camera-toting conventioneers. Bhutan's monarchy conferred with some of the world's tourism experts; and, in consultation with their own people, developed policies that are found nowhere else.

Knowing that Bhutan's GDP was around $1,900 per person, I knew I'd be traveling to a poor country. Imagine my surprise when I discovered not a developing world, but 'Another' world, one with lessons for all economies.

Bhutan controls the way in which people visit. You must go with a tour guide and there is a minimum tariff. As I write this, the tariff is $200US per person per day. "That's expensive!" a friend exclaimed when I explained the structure. "Not really," I replied, "That includes your hotel, meals, guide and ground transportation. How much did you spend per day on your last trip to Europe?" Silence fell as the truth sunk in.

This system is more than a minimum price guided tour. You pay your money to the government and only when you leave the country satisfied, does the tour company receive your payment. Talk about an incentive to deliver great customer service!

Because of the payment structure, guides are more than storytellers. "Guides have a lot of power in Bhutan," Lotay Richan, cofounder of Bridge to Bhutan, says. "If a hotel or restaurant doesn't provide good rooms or food, the guide will just say that the clients are complaining too much and move them to another business."

The policy that underpins this system is visionary. It ensures that tour operators receive a fair price; there is no race to the bottom with price-cutting. Tourists get a better experience because they are traveling with guides who can afford extra training.

The environment benefits because tourists are guided so they are less likely to engage in harmful behavior. Tourists are also coached on cultural norms so they don't offend locals or inadvertently damage religious sites.

For a country with some impressive mountains, there is no mountain climbing. For a time, Bhutan allowed foreigners to climb its peaks, much like Nepal to the west. Farmers complained climbers were upsetting the deities and crops were failing. Responding to these concerns in a way seldom seen in the west, climbing was stopped. So now visitors to Bhutan hike around the mountains, but they don't climb them. The government policies value cultural preservation over foreign currency.

There are other policies for sustainability. The constitution requires sixty percent of the country's forest be preserved. Only the government can log trees and they use selective logging. All architecture conforms to traditional styles. Gross National Happiness (GNH) is the measure of progress, not GDP.

When I explain Bhutan's unique policies, the usual response is "That's fine for them, but we couldn't do something like that in the West!" Maybe it is time to ask, "Why not?" There are differences between Bhutan and Canada's political, social and economic landscapes, but there are lessons to be learned, especially when it comes to putting long-term communal interests ahead of individual short-term satisfaction.

Policies Worthy of Superheroes

Policies are also important for businesses. You might not have thought about policies, but they can have real impacts on your work conditions and the way you are asked to approach your job.

My sister Brenda works for SaskEnergy, rated one of the best 100 Employers in Canada. They encourage their staff to build skills with a wide range of training programs and tuition subsidies. Since she went to work for SaskEnergy, Brenda has completed her Certified Internal Auditor designation and enjoys traveling the continent teaching other auditors. The company gives her time off to teach because they can earn training credits for other employees.

If you work for Mountain Equipment Co-op, you can be proud knowing it donates a minimum of one percent of sales to conservation activities; for every sale you make, you are supporting environmental causes. Other companies offer sabbaticals, on-site farmer's market, concierge services, artists in residence, same-sex partner benefits or the chance to bring man's best friend to work. Google is one of a growing number of companies that lets employees to bring their dogs to work.

So next time you find yourself muttering about your work conditions or the decisions of your manager, put your thinking cap on. Are there new policies that would improve the situation? Do your research and bring it up at your next staff meeting. Companies love to discover daredevils within their ranks. They need innovative ideas to stay competitive and each of us can contribute.

Lesson #9

Take Your Cape on Vacation

In comic books superheroes are too busy fighting evil to take time off. To a twelve-year old reader, that seemed logical. Since I've been working for several decades, I know that all work and no play makes for a boring, burned-out accountant or lawyer or ecotourism consultant. Time off is important for each of us.

Employees consider vacation time to be one of their most important benefits, but yet a quarter of people don't take their full allotment. Apparently, we're afraid of being replaced by another superhero or we are so darn dedicated we think the place will stop if we aren't at our desks.

And yet our economy is based increasingly on service jobs. These jobs require us to be creative, and being creative requires energy. Or at least it comes easier. Total exhaustion can lead to brilliant moments of innovation, like when you realize no one really reads your monthly report because you forgot to send it after working on an all-nighter deadline. But, more often, working too much leads to mistakes on the job and at home. People who don't take enough leisure time have more health problems and unhappier marriages than people who hit the road regularly.

So if you haven't been making vacation a priority in your life, rethink that decision. You can create some memories with your kids, remember how to laugh at silly things, and recharge your batteries. You may even spark a new interest or way of looking at old problems.

Reentry Suggestions

Often the big changes that come from travel don't happen on the trip. You take the holiday, have fun (or not) and come home. That's when the real personal growth starts. You find your old lifestyle or your way of getting things done doesn't fit anymore.

Maybe your house looks better than ever, but you realize your passive-aggressive coworker is making you sick. Or that 'friend' who constantly regales you with another tale of woe isn't just going through a difficult time, but is just plain selfish. It's time to kick them to the curb and focus on the activities and people that replenish you, renew you and are just plain fun!

Just back from a big trip, you may be tempted to quit your job before lunch on the first day, but don't! You might need that paycheque for your next trip, but something more important is going on. Those feelings of dissatisfaction are precious jewels, glimmers of light in the darkness.

Re-entry to your life after a vacation is often uncomfortable, but exploring your feelings for a day or two will show you where the tension points are in your life. Like a pair of shoes that pinch or rub, coming back from a trip will show you where your life has gotten too small or where you have settled for the cheap, knock-off experiences.

Keep track of your first day grumblings. I've learned to fly a plane, rock climb and drum as a result of those gritty Monday mornings after a great trip.

You will not make tough decisions when you're feeling good so remember: pain can be your friend. I doubt anyone has started a career change while swilling Mai Tais on a South Pacific beach. But I know more than one person, myself included, have changed careers when holiday experiences were compared to everyday realities and found lacking.

To get the most out of your time off, embrace the re-entry process and look for new ideas during this fertile time. Don't start a trip thinking you'll come home a better, fitter, kinder person after a week away. You are probably too sleep deprived to do more than try a new item on the dinner menu.

Relax, enjoy your trip while you become a slug on the beach or the mountain, and give your inner wisdom a chance to be heard. Deep down, each of has the answers, we just need time for solutions to percolate to the top, and the sanity to recognize them.

Travel gives you time and space to create these changes; going home to your 'real life' reveals them. Think of it like baking a cake. The trip is the shopping and mixing of the ingredients. Your creation forms while you travel and when you get home, you reveal the finished product. It isn't a cake, but a better version of you. Travel isn't the only way to know yourself better, but it's one of the most fun.

Life Changing Adventures

A safari to Africa introduced me to ecotourism and started me on a career transformation. Other people have found trips lead to big changes in their businesses. In February 2004, Peter Seligmann, co-founder and ECO of Conservation International, was on a private trip to Costa Rican's Coco Island National Park, with Samuel Robson (Rob) Walton, eldest son of the Wal-Mart founder.

The Walton's family foundation had been active in conservation before, but Peter impressed upon Rob how much more influence he could have on environmental protection if Wal-Mart could influence its vast customer base.

In 2005, Wal-Mart unveiled its sustainability initiatives that were aimed at improving energy efficiency, reducing waste and selling sustainable products. Although we may more often associate Wal-Mart with low prices than going green, their size means small changes can have big environmental effects.

Wal-Mart's Executive Vice-President Rollin Ford estimated in 2007 that if they were able to improve their supply chain efficiency so they were out of stock of less often, they could reduce extra trips. "On a daily basis, more than 24 million people shop at our stores. If 100,000 extra trips are avoided by having items in stock, we will save customers $22.8 million a year in gas savings and reduce greenhouse gases by 80,209 tonnes."

Perhaps, Wal-Mart's move to a greener world was inevitable in face of changing social values, but I like to think leisure time for its leaders led to a paradigm shift and that time off is time well spent!

Lesson #10

Believe in Daredevils

Hopefully you are feeling excited about your future. If you are not sure you are up to daredevil activities or don't know where to start, just take one small step, even if it's trying something different for breakfast every day for a week!

After I broke my ankle hiking in Bhutan, I was deeply demoralized when I got back on my exercise bike after the cast was removed. With the best of intentions, I managed to do only fifteen seconds before my leg was worn out.

"Fifteen seconds!" I screamed to myself, "How am I ever going to get back to normal if I can only bike fifteen seconds at a time!" That's when my trusty accounting background came in handy. I told myself, "If I can do fifteen seconds today and if I can double it tomorrow, that will be thirty seconds. If I keep increasing by fifteen or thirty seconds, I'll be up to two or three minutes by the end of a week. And that could be parlayed into fifteen or twenty minutes in a month."

And that is what I did. My doctors thought cross-country skiing was out of my winter plans unless the snow stayed until April. I was skiing flat sections by the end of January. And so every time I walk by that exercise bike, I think of how far fifteen seconds can take you. What can you do in fifteen seconds?

If All Superheroes Believe

The grey whales that spend their summers along Canada's west coast mate and give birth in the sheltered lagoons of Mexico's Baja Peninsula. Until the 1920s the whales were hunted in these shallow lagoons. It was easy picking for the whalers in the shallow waters where the whales were concentrated. The waters ran red with whales' blood; the whalers called the whales devilfish as they fought back during the slaughter, smashing boats and hurling people into the water.

Fortunately, whaling in these waters has ended and the Mexican government is protecting the marine life. The Whale Sanctuary of El Vizcaino was designated a biosphere in 1993. Salt mining competes with whales for habitat in the area. To head off the conflict the Mexican government bought a fifty-one percent interest in Mitsubishi's salt mine operations in the area. This ensures that these sensitive areas remain for generations to come.

A visit to these waters was on my bucket list and I was thrilled to find a company – Baja Airventures – that made it easy to get there. With small planes flying direct from San Diego to the Sea of Cortez, I was soon on a small panga (boat) in a whale watching Mecca. I felt like Linda Blair in the Exorcist as my head swiveled to see the numerous whale spouts scattered across the lagoon.

"There have been reports of 'friendlies' in the area," Fred, our guide, explained. The excitement level in the group went up as Fred had earlier; explained that a 'friendly' was a whale that approached the boats, sometimes close enough to be touched. I hoped I might be lucky enough to touch a whale.

On our second day with the whales we met our most memorable 'friendlies'. It was a mother and her calf, and I guess she regarded us as the rubber ducks in the whales' version of a bathtub. She brought her calf over to the boat to frolic in the prop wash, and to look at the strange creatures in the boat. The mother and her calf bobbed near my husband's side of the boat.

I was envious that I wasn't closer, but managed to tamp down the little green monster, as I filmed his special moment. The whale calf emerged from the water inches from my husband. "I reached out to touch it, and just when I was going to reach it, the whale pulled back just an inch," he enthused." I didn't touch a whale, but I touched its aura!!"

Our boat was filled with much chattering and laughing as reflected on our close encounter with a beast big enough to send us into the drink if so inclined. I was humbled by the forgiveness this species showed in spite of past transgressions by humans.

Proof that great change is possible when enough daredevils want something to happen! What would you like the next generation to remember from your efforts?

Superheroes Adapt and Try Again

As you start to make changes in your personal or professional life, no doubt things will not go according to plan. You will find that you don't like your new hobby as much as you expected, or you may discover an unexpected income source.

When I started advertising my book, ***Reinventure: How Travel Adventure Can Change Your Life***, I felt there was opportunity in opening people's eyes to the transformative power of travel. I was surprised I'd overlooked a bigger prospect.

"Are you one of us?" asked the email from the Canadian Institute of Chartered Accountants. "We saw a newspaper article about your book and it mentioned how you started as an accountant. We are looking for Chartered Accountants with interesting stories for our newsletter."

I noticed that the media had been interested in this angle, as if it was the most surprising thing in the world that an accountant had turned into an 'interesting person'.

"I started in the CA Program," I replied, "But I'm now a CMA. Are you still interested?" The reply was helpful, "No, but you should contact your association. They also look for stories of accountants doing interesting work."

I was pleasantly surprised at how quickly I got a reply from the CMA newsletter editor, and plans were underway for a cover story. It was great publicity and led to additional exposure when they used my story in their national marketing program.

I had never thought that my transformation from accountant to strategic planner was particularly newsworthy; but it turns out it is. And it has led to a new line of speaking engagements, and to this book. What new opportunities have you found when something failed? Have you ever found an unexpected way to make money? If not keep looking, they are out there.

The Daredevil Wish

Hopefully the lessons I shared from the daredevils I've met will reinvigorate you and spark ideas on how you can live your best life. We are lucky to live in a time and place where there is freedom and the means to pursue our interests, no matter how obscure or cutting-edge.

So go forth like your favorite superhero. Put on a crazy outfit, learn to fly, develop superhuman abilities or at least learn a few party tricks that make it look like you did. You will have more laughs, and enjoy the people in your life more. Chances are they will like you better too!

Learning a new recipe for zucchini may not win you the Nobel Peace Prize, but you may spark a change that leaves you feeling like a prizewinner. It isn't the big leaps of faith that create the biggest splashes; it is the everyday heroes stepping forward each day, doing the small things with pride and enthusiasm (real or faked) that make the journey worthwhile.

Have fun in tights and drop me a line with your best adventures!

"With great power, comes great responsibilities"
Spiderman

When You Need a New Cape

By now, hopefully a daredevil is stirring inside of you. For most of you, that enthusiasm for new discoveries will put a new spring in your step and you will look at your job, your family, your friends with new eyes; and you'll like what you see. Some of you may decide you need to change your job or your occupation. This next section is for you.

I did it. You can do it too. Creating a career in an unconventional field can be hard, but it is possible. When I started my transition from accountant to ecotourism planner there were no manuals to point the way. There were few jobs in the field; none in the city that I chose to call home. Fortunately, I stumbled upon a delightful book – **Wishcraft** by Barbara Sher – that explained how you could take what you loved and turn it into a living. I was hooked by the concept and, while it wasn't easy, I kept at it.

I talked to anyone who could tell me more about this emerging field, and I spent hours considering how my business skills could be transferred into a field abounding with biologists, policy wonks, public relations experts and marketing professionals.

I eventually carved a niche as a conduit of information to help sustainable tourism operators succeed without being chained to their laptops.

I will share the tools I used to create an unconventional career with few signposts to guide the way. Chances are you are looking for work in a field that is still evolving. In looking for work that gives you time doing what you like and reasonable pay, you may run into dead-ends reading the want ads or searching the Internet. I'll share what I've learned and help you find the way.

You may be disappointed with some of what you discover in your search and you will probably work harder than you've ever worked before, but if you persevere you **will** find a way to combine your life's passions and a living. Let's get started!

A.   What Do You Want To Do?

Creating an unconventional career like the Daredevils in this book will require you to be creative, persistent and clever. You will also need a level of self-awareness so you can find the opportunities likely to keep you happy.

Everyone has different interests and the trick will be finding a moneymaking opportunity connected to yours. There will be more possibilities that you might think. You may have to discard some of them based upon your family situation or your tolerance for risk, but for now focus on what you want to have more of in your life.

Start by listing your goals. What do you want to get out of your career? A chance to spend more time in a favorite recreational activity? More time outdoors? These are common goals, but make sure to consider the people you hope to include in these goals.

If you want to spend more time canoeing, are you ready to do with it with people who don't know an eddy from a riptide? Many people are surprised at how little time they actually have left over for their sport or interest once they have taken care of the business of customer safety, equipment selection, training and, of course, accounting.

Will you want to work for someone else or are you prepared to take on the risks of self-employment? Lots of people envy the flexibility of a business owner, but overlook the hours that go into getting a business up and running. Be honest about the time and energy you can commit to getting your new career established.

Where do you want to spend your time? Is it important for you to be located in a certain part of the country? Are you mobile? Tourism, like many businesses, is seasonal and you will have to find something to do in the off season. One option may be to do the same thing, but in a different hemisphere. Paddling guides have been doing this for years. After leading trips in North America all summer, they relocate to Central America or Southeast Asia for the winter months.

To help clarify what you want in a career, try answering the following questions.

My goals for a career are:

1._____

2._____

3._____

4._____

5._____

The kind of people I would like to work with include: (describe each briefly)

Customers: _____

Coworkers: _____

Boss: _____

I would like to do the following types of tasks and activities:

1. _____

2. _____

3. _____

4. _____

What type of physical environment do you want to work in?

_____

What work hours would you prefer? Do you like shift work? Long hours? Flexibility?

_____

What level of income do you need to cover your living expenses? If you are married, have you discussed your income goals with your partner to make sure they support your goals and expectations?

_____

B.   Are You Ready For The Challenges?

Defining your goals will often take several days or weeks as you mull over your options and find the time to answer the earlier questions honestly. Once you have a general idea of what you would like to do, start investigating the jobs and business opportunities found in the fields that interest you.

You may find opportunities working in the public sector or in private businesses. If you are deeply concerned about social or environmental causes you might like working with a non-profit or non-government organization (NGO).

Some career paths may be obvious, but there are probably many you are unaware of. For example, in ecotourism, people might think of being a kayak guide or running a B&B catering to bird watchers, but there are other careers that you may have overlooked. Insurance agents, accountants, lawyers and other professionals are also needed. You might want to consider working in one of these fields and specializing in a topic in which you are interested.

Do an inventory of all the organizations in your community that may have a connection to activities you find interesting. Try to list names of organizations operating in your area. These may be potential employers, but equally as important they will have people that can provide useful information for your career search.

Once you've completed the inventory of your community, spend some time on the Internet. Visit the websites of the organizations that interest you. Learn about their goals and the types of activities they undertake. Read their press releases or online newsletters. What type of challenges do they face? Showing up with solutions to these problems can give you an instant leg up in establishing your career.

After you've investigated a dozen different organizations summarize your thoughts below:

Which organizations were most interesting?

1. _____

2. _____

3. _____

4. _____

5. _____

What aspects of these organizations did I like the most?

1. _____

2. _____

3. _____

4. _____

Were there things these organizations had in common? For example, were they all committed to delivering quality service? Did they focus on social goals or giving back to the community? Was there an aspect of their commitment to lifelong learning that excited you? Try to summarize the elements that struck a chord with you.

_____

What common challenges did you see with these organizations? For example, were many of them looking to attract younger customers or wanting to expand their shoulder season activities?

_____

What ideas do you have on how these organizations can beat these challenges?

_____

C.   What Do You Bring To The Party?

Now that you have a better idea of what you want to do and the types of organizations that interest you, it is time to look at what you can offer.

This can be a difficult process for some people. They may feel that they have no applicable skills or training. I can relate to that. Trained as a professional accountant I wasn't sure my skills would be valued in the ecotourism field. However, I had been building bridges to a new career without realizing it and I suspect you have too!

As I described earlier in the book, before my career change I had been indulging my passion for wildlife by being a volunteer guide at the Calgary Zoo. I had developed new skills in interpretation, public speaking and wildlife viewing. With my understanding of the newly emerging field of ecotourism, I could see that many organizations needed people with good communication skills, knowledge of business processes, and an interest in people. Those were things I could provide and you will find you have skills that can be 'repackaged' to create the career you want.

Start by listing those skills you possess that will be of immediate value in a new industry or position. This might include any certifications, diplomas or licenses you've picked up in your pursuit of your passion.

Add to the list the skills you have that do not come with certifications. For example, lots of tourism organizations need people with specialized knowledge to add interest to their customers' trips, so if you are a crack birder or have the Aboriginal history of your community researched, write it down. You would be amazed at how many people are looking for someone with your background, even if it is on a part-time basis.

List any degrees, diplomas or certifications you hold even if they aren't directly related to your field of interest. You may find a way to link your knowledge to this field or do online training to add a specialization in your area of interest.

Tourism employers have told me time and again that they can teach an employee almost anything, but they can't teach a person to smile. If you have the ability to chitchat with people or make them feel comfortable in a social situation, you will do well in many fields. These 'soft' skills are often most important in determining your overall success in tourism; other industries value them as well.

List those skills or attributes you possess that may help you with your career. Be sure to include your ability to organize, remain calm under pressure, build entire structures using duct tape and one fallen tree, etc.

D.   Tell Me More

At this point you have a good idea of what you can contribute to an organization and you have some idea of your goals. It's time for you to get out and find out more about jobs or unconventional career paths in your community. You are about to start on the informational interviewing process.

This wonderful tool is described by Richard Nelson Bolles in **What Color is Your Parachute?** as the **single** most important tool you can use in your career building process. Want to find out more about jobs in your field? Use information interviews. Want to find out who might be hiring? Use information interviews. Want to find out what associations the movers and shakers belong to? Use information interviews.

The premise of an information interview is that you ask an industry professional for fifteen to twenty minutes to get an expert opinion on issues you are researching. It is not a job search!!! You want to find out more about the field before you decide which organizations are worthy of your time, talents and your resume.

Go to these interviews with questions on the main issues facing these organizations, what types of skills their employees possess, what they are missing, and which trade associations they belong to. This will help you understand how to best position your skills **before** you apply for a job. You may decide based upon your informational interviews that you have been looking in the wrong places and need to redirect your search or develop new skills. Or that self-employment is a better route.

Start by identifying five organizations where you would like an informational interview. Ask everyone you know for the names of anyone remotely associated with your interest area and call them up for appointments. Explain carefully why you want to see them so they don't mistake you for a job hunter. Eventually you will be looking for work, but at this point you are just researching your options.

Conduct your informational interviews. Respect people's time and keep to the twenty minutes originally requested. Send a thank you note. It will help you build your new career network. If you are having trouble finding people in your community with the career you want, look farther afield. Sometimes people are more willing to share information with someone located at a distance because they are less likely to be seen as a competitor.

What observations can you make about your targeted industry or field since you concluded your interviews?

Has your research given you ideas on what your future career might look like? Describe what form your career possibilities might take. Will this be a job in the conventional sense or will it be a variety of jobs linked together to give you the income you need? Maybe you will be working with a number of employers to create year round employment or you may be creating a business to provide yourself with self-employment income.

What other information do you need before you apply for work or start a business? Do you need to research zoning guidelines? Find out what training or certifications are offered in your community? Make a list of things you need to know and where you might get the information.

E. Making Friends and Building Your Network

Hopefully the informational interviewing process showed you the value of networking and you added a few names to your address book. If not, now is the time to build a professional network. Many industries are made up of social individuals. Your ability to succeed will be determined to a large extent by how good you are at building relationships with people. While you are building your career prospects, take the time to build the network that will generate the job offers or business partnerships you will need for success.

Your Internet research and information interviews should reveal which associations the people in your field belong to. Join up and be prepared to attend conferences. They are a great place to build your network. It is a low stress, fun-filled way to meet people and, if you are still finishing off your education, organizers often have special student's rates. I know of lots of people, myself included, who have gotten major breaks through the casual connections made at conferences.

F. Finding the Opportunity

Now is time to start looking for the job of your dreams. Using the information you gathered in your informational interviews, decide how you can help organizations solve their problems. The fact that you have taken the time to research their company and suggest success strategies will set you far above the competition.

Call your contacts and tell them what type of job you are now looking for. Don't be shy. Tell everyone what type of position you want AND what you have to offer. Your information interviews will have given you a much better idea of which companies you want to work for. You will also have a clearer idea of what skills employers are looking for. Chances are you will also have personal contacts that can keep your resume from disappearing in the Human Resource's pool of unsolicited applicants.

You may decide that working for someone else is not for you. Many people wanting into the field of ecotourism and adventure travel will decide to start their own businesses. If this option interests you, consider working for a similar business to gain some experience before you invest your savings in a business. Once you've seen how ecotourism businesses operate, you can move forward with your ides. My book, ***The Business of Ecotourism*** can help you create the vision and the business plan you need to develop your concept further.

Don't get discouraged. It will take time to land the perfect job or build a business. You may need to start with a less than perfect job and work your way into the position or company of your dreams. Having a good attitude while you 'earn your stripes' will endear you to employers and make your journey go much faster. If it helps, read motivational books or watch motivational DVDs. Looking for work is the hardest job there is, so be kind to yourself. Things will come together if you are persistent.

G.   Increasing Your Chances of Success

When you are building your new career in emerging industries recognize that it will take time to become established the same way as in more traditional fields. For example, in tourism, very few people work year round in this field. Most people have secondary sources of income in the off-season. Some people take their marketing expertise and design websites for other companies. Some people find complementary outdoor jobs with lots of flexibility like firefighting. Others look for work they can do from home, for example, building furniture.

If you think you'll have slow times, find other work to smooth the bumps. Are there skills you already possess that can generate extra income? Are there certifications or licenses you can add that will provide financial security during down cycles?

Don't feel that you have failed if you need other ways to support your true passions while you establish yourself. Many people spend years building up their businesses to where they can rely on it for their annual livelihood. Having another source of income gives you time to realize your career dreams. If you keep at it, one day people will be telling you they envy your lifestyle. Even though you will be working like a demon, you'll look up and realize that you've made it!

H.   Giving Back

Building your unconventional career will require the help of others. As I've suggested, asking established professionals for information interviews will be an important part of your strategy. Some people will be extremely generous of their time and help with contacts that will prove invaluable. Remember to 'pay it forward'. Once you've got your toehold established, take the time to help others follow their dreams.

If someone calls you for an informational interview, help him or her if you can. Give a student the chance to work for you on a co-op work term. Donate your time to an industry association. Doing these things will strengthen your industry and build a community with passionate, talented individuals.

Be sure as well to take time to recharge and spend time in nature. You will find creating your career time-consuming and there is a temptation to give up some of your favorite activities. Make it a priority to get out in the woods, mountains, desert or waters that rejuvenate you. You'll be happier and your contribution to your new industry will be greater!

I leave you a closing thought by John Muir

"Climb the mountains and get their good tidings.
Nature's peace will flow into you as sunshine flows into trees.
The winds will blow their own freshness into you...
while cares will drop off like autumn leaves."

About the Author

Carol Patterson is a tourism planner who travels the world helping people, communities and businesses develop their nature tourism destinations. Her company, Kalahari Management Inc., has been providing strategic planning, tourism assessments and training since 1991. Carol is much sought after as a speaker as she weaves her stories through lessons for growth and renewal. Carol has been to Africa seven times, Borneo three times and Iceland four times, and has yet to lose a piece of luggage. A winner of a 2007 Woman of Vision award, she lives in Calgary, Alberta, with her husband, horse and cats.

Book Clubs

For those of you in book clubs, the following questions can be used to generate discussion around *Accountants and Other Daredevils.*

1. What themes are common among the various daredevils described in the book? Do you notice any common characteristics? Are there people you know who would be daredevils?

2. What barriers do you think prevent people from taking risks?

3. How do parents encourage their children to take risks? How might they make their children risk-adverse? How aware are parents of the biases they instill in their children?

4. Does our current culture encourage people to be more innovative? What risks are regarded favorably? What types of risk-taking are frowned upon by society?

5. Do companies foster a culture of innovation? Why would they want daredevils working for them? How can they encourage people to live their best lives while meeting their corporate goals?

6. What events or milestones have occurred in your community due to the efforts of a small group of people? What sets these people apart from others? Do you think some communities attract people with daredevil attitudes or do daredevils shape their environment to suit their needs?

Know a Closet Superhero?

Help Your Loved Ones, Friends and Colleagues
Discover the Daredevil Within

Check Your Local Bookstore or Order Here

For credit card or International orders, please call 1-800-232-4444 or
visit www.trafford.com

Canadian Orders	*U.S. Orders*
For each copy, send a Money Order for $25.94 ($18.99 + 95¢ GST + $6 S&H)	For each copy, send a Postal Money Order for $28.99 ($18.99 + $10 S&H)

Direct orders:
Please send me _____ copies of *Accountants and Other Daredevils*
My cheque or money order for $_____ is enclosed.

Name: _____

Organization:_____

Mailing Address:_____

City/Province or State/ Postal Code or ZIP:

_____

_____

Phone: _____ Email: _____

Mail to:

Kalahari Management Inc.
PO Box 46056, Inglewood RPO
Calgary, Alberta, Canada T2G 5H7

Email: info@kalahari-online.com
Visit our website for more information on Daredevils
www.otherdaredevils.com
Author is available for speaking engagements